Preface

ADecadeLater – Why We Need to Think DigitalMoreThan Ever

In 2015, Think Digital was born out of a simple but urgent belief: businesses that fail to embrace digital transformation would risk becoming irrelevant. A decade later, that belief has not only been proven true; it's now turbocharged by a new force: Artificial Intelligence.

When I first wrote this book, "digital" meant getting online, streamlining workflows, and staying ahead of changing customer expectations. Today, it means all that, and so much more. From Agentic AI handling complex workflows to predictive analytics shaping decisions before they're made, the digital frontier has shifted dramatically. But the core principles remain: transformation is not about tech, it's about mindset, execution, and above all, people.

This updated edition: Think Digital: Rewired for the AI Age, is my way of revisiting those timeless ideas, now seen through a sharper, smarter lens. Whether you're an SME owner, a startup founder, or a corporate leader, the playbook has expanded. The rules have evolved. And the urgency? It's even greater.

So here's to the next chapter in our digital journey. Let's not just think digital. Let's do digital, intelligently.

- Logan Nathan
Melbourne, 2025

Acknowledgments

This book is the result of a collective effort, and I am deeply grateful to those who helped bring it to life.

First, I thank my wife and life partner, Nimmie Nathan, for her unwavering support throughout this journey. A special thanks to my customers, staff, and suppliers at i4T Global and solomoIT, whose trust and collaboration over the past 22 years provided invaluable insights.

I also want to acknowledge Wardah Wadood, our Product Growth Marketing Strategist, for her strategic input, and Saalik Ahamed, our Product Marketer, whose design expertise and passion for AI helped shape this book.

I'm also grateful to the visionary founders who generously shared their industry-specific insights, shaping this book with their real-world expertise and dedication to AI-driven innovation.

Finally, to the broader team and community who have contributed ideas, feedback, and encouragement along the way, your support has made this work possible.

Epilogue

A Personal Note from the Author

Thank you for walking this journey with me, and what a journey it has been! Many fundamentals have evolved since I published my first book in 2015, and it makes me wonder what the next ten years will bring.

No one could have predicted the impact AI would have on digital transformation as we see it today. What's next in the coming decade? As a digital enthusiast, I'll certainly be watching, though my energy and interest in playing a part remain to be seen.

As a serial entrepreneur, with my current venture being i4T Global, much of what I've shared in this book comes directly from the hands-on experiences of my passionate team.

We've spent years learning, testing, and refining the end-to-end processes SMEs need to thrive, and embedding those lessons into the i4T Global ecosystem.

When I first began helping small and medium businesses more than 2 decades ago, embracing digital transformation, it was an uphill battle. Many didn't see the value. Some believed it was only meant for the "big players." But over time, I've had the privilege of witnessing so many SMEs rise, evolve, and take the lead in ways they never imagined.

What continues to inspire me is the moment when we realise that we are not just adapting to the future; we're helping create it. That we are building something our customers trust, our teams take pride in, and our communities benefit from. Something meaningful.

And it's no longer just about business.

In this AI-powered, digital-first world, opportunities are emerging for everyone, from educators and artists to local tradespeople, healthcare workers, and even retirees launching passion projects. Those who were once considered "non-tech-savvy" are now automating tasks, expanding their reach, and making a real impact, often in places we never expected.

I hope this book has served as a roadmap, a spark, and perhaps even a source of courage for us to take the next bold step.

My next book, however, will focus on my personal life journey, which has largely been learning IT and digital transformation for over four decades. I'll certainly be referencing how these influences have shaped me over the past 45 years.

Until then, let's stay curious and bold! And build a business, and a life, that truly matters. To us, to our people, and to the world around us.

Table of Contents

Preface

Acknowledgments

Epilogue

Chapter 1:
The Foundation – Then   01

Chapter 2:
AI-First Thinking   13

Chapter 3:
Hyper-Personalisation in the Age of AI   25

Chapter 4:
No-Code / Low-Code Empowerment for Teams   44

Chapter 5:
Agentic Systems: The Rise of Autonomous Workflows   53

Chapter 6:
Continuous Learning as a Digital Culture   69

Chapter 7:
Digital Maturity Self-Assessment   85

Chapter 8:
90-Day AI Adoption Roadmap for SMEs   101

Chapter 9:
Top Tools for 2025 and Beyond   115

Chapter 10:
Case Studies: Lessons from the Frontlines   132

Chapter 11:
The Role of Leadership in a Digital Future   143

Chapter 12:
From Survival to Significance: What's Next for Digital-First Businesses   153

Chapter 13:
Real Insights from the AI Frontier   161

Chapter 14:
Closing Reflections: Building a Business That Adapts, Learns, and Leads   176

References   182

Appendices   184

Chapter 1:

The Foundation – Then

Before we look ahead, we must understand where we started.

Think Digital – The Ultimate Transformation Guide for Businesses was born in a pretty defining time.

Back in 2015, businesses everywhere were waking up to a simple truth: going digital wasn't just a nice-to-have. It was the bedrock. What we explored back then weren't just shiny new tricks; it was a whole new way of thinking.

That first book went on to help thousands of SMEs and entrepreneurs across Australia and beyond reimagine how they connect, operate, and grow in a digital world.

Of course, the world's moved on since. What once felt ground-breaking is now the baseline.

So this chapter is a look back at those core lessons that sparked the first big wave of digital change. They're the foundations we're still building on today, and the springboard for what's next.

Tech-Ready Mindset

Cultivate a digital-first way of thinking. It's not just about using tools; it's about rewiring beliefs, behaviours, and business models.

A decade ago, the big word on everyone's lips was "transformation."

Digital wasn't just an add-on anymore; it had become essential. But while most businesses were busy launching websites, setting up Facebook pages, or firing off email campaigns, only a few truly understood what this transformation demanded.

The original Think Digital was written to help close that gap. Not with fancy theory, but with stories from the trenches. It was never just about tools or campaigns; it was about flipping how we think. A mindset shift. One that even back then, was absolutely non-negotiable.

We banged on a lot about the need to "think digital." Not as a buzzword, but as a genuine call to arms. Because back then, plenty of businesses treated digital like a side project. Something for the marketing team to sort out, or a job to handball to an agency. But the smart ones realised digital wasn't a box to tick; rather, it was a new way of thinking. A cultural shift. A fresh lens for making decisions.

The Digital mindset Shift

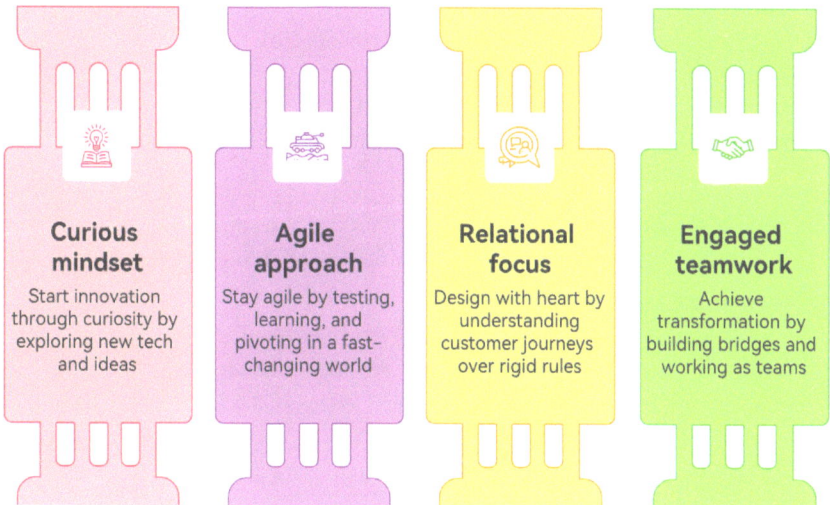

Curious mindset	Agile approach	Relational focus	Engaged teamwork
Start innovation through curiosity by exploring new tech and ideas	Stay agile by testing, learning, and pivoting in a fast-changing world	Design with heart by understanding customer journeys over rigid rules	Achieve transformation by building bridges and working as teams

What we didn't fully grasp then, but could sense in our guts, was that digital wasn't just changing how we did business. It was reshaping what business itself would look like.

Every chat about growth, marketing, hiring, delivery, and value was starting to change. And it all came back to mindset.

We were stepping away from a static, shout-at-the-crowd world of print ads and cold calls, and into a dynamic, two-way world of interaction, feedback, data, and meaning.

For so many Aussie SMEs, full of gutsy innovators, grafters, and dreamers, this was a massive shift. The challenge wasn't just finding product-market fit anymore; it was getting digitally fit.

Were we ready to lead in a world shaped by tech, driven by rising customer expectations, and influenced by global trends?

That question needed a mindset to answer it. And that was the real bedrock of digital transformation.

It's why that first book hammered home the idea of thinking digital, because without that shift upstairs, every tactic was just noise.

Human-Centric Transformation

Put people at the heart of every change. From customers to employees, experience is the new battleground.

In Think Digital, we pushed a big, simple idea: don't start with your product, start with your people. Not just the ones on your payroll, but the folks outside, your customers, your community, your soon-to-be champions.

Sounds obvious now, but rewind to 2015, and most businesses were still product-first, campaign-focused, and stuck in broadcast mode. What Think Digital did, and what struck a chord with SMEs across the country, was flip the script. We asked businesses to see themselves through their customers' eyes.

We talked about human-centric transformation, not as a fluffy marketing ideal, but as a must-have structural shift.

The framework we laid out in Chapter 2 of the original book stepped through how to get into your customer's mindset, shape a brand story that means something, and engage through rich, multi-sensory storytelling, sight, sound, and feel.

And it worked. Not because it was trendy, but because it was deeply human.

Think of Nike's "Make It Count" campaign we unpacked in that first book. It wasn't just slick video work. It tapped straight into customer aspirations. Nike didn't just sell tech; they sold belief. They invited people to be part of the brand's energy, turning simple movement into something meaningful. That's customer-centricity done right.

Or Airbnb, which didn't just fill empty rooms; they rewrote the rules of trust and hospitality. Their magic? Knowing their users inside out. From using Craigslist to launch, to telling powerful visual stories worldwide, Airbnb was a clinic in reverse-engineering the customer's emotional (and practical) journey.

Those core takeaways still hit home. Remember SEE:

Customer-focused strategies

Evoke emotional experiences
Build experiences that evoke emotions, making people feel rather than just notice

Empower customer storytelling
Let customers tell your story since they are the most credible storytellers available

Solve customer problems
Focus on solving actual problems that customers truly care about instead of emphasizing features

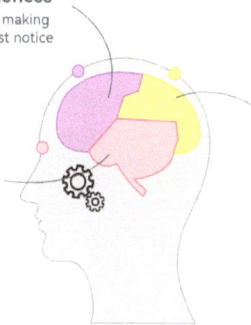

Customer-centric transformation isn't about having a customer service desk. It's about building a business that listens, adapts, and evolves around the people it serves. It's moving from inside-out shouting ("Here's what we do") to outside-in experience design ("Here's how we make your life better, simpler, smarter").

The brand story framework we shared, digging into customer pain points, showing unique value, and delivering emotional resonance, became how so many SMEs learned to humanise their online presence.

It was never about chasing viral hits. It was about showing you're in sync with your audience. That you get them. That you're on their side.

That pivot, from broadcasting to belonging, is what set up everything else that's come in the digital transformation journey.

Integrate Technology with Purpose

Adopt tech with intention, not hype. Use the right tools the right way, to solve real problems and unlock new possibilities.

In that early digital wave, tech was both a lighthouse and a lure.

Everywhere you looked, there was a new tool, platform, or trend promising to change the game. It was equal parts thrilling and overwhelming. For heaps of businesses, especially SMEs, it was easy to mix up busyness with strategy, to think that starting a Facebook page or installing a CRM meant they were "digital."
But here's the truth: tech only helps if it helps you.

The smart operators didn't chase every fad. They started with clarity. What problem are we solving? What do our customers need? What's stopping us from doing it better?

When used with purpose, tech was a lever, driving efficiency, scale, personalisation, and reach. Without a strategy, it was just clutter.

What stood out was that the most effective businesses weren't the ones neck-deep in every shiny tool. They were picky. They used tech to lift human experiences, not replace them. Tech was the helper, not the hero.

5

Nokia's "QWERTY Me" campaign is a cracking example.[2] Its brilliance wasn't about flashy specs. It was about picking the right platforms for their crowd. They knew their customers were mobile-first, social, and big on local. So they harnessed SMS, Facebook, WhatsApp, plus on-ground events to make it sing. They joined the dots: online with offline, tech with community, content with culture.

This was digital done right; purpose, platform, and people in perfect harmony.

Another big shift? Businesses started seeing the whole chessboard. Digital wasn't just marketing anymore. It touched sales, service, hiring, ops, and customer support. The clever ones stitched their tools together, building systems that talked, scaled, and flexed.

And then the mobile exploded. If you weren't in your customer's pocket, you were out of the game. Websites became mobile-first. Content loaded faster, looked sharper, spoke clearer.

Yet through all the tech noise, the golden rule stuck: don't chase tech. Choose tech that helps you serve, grow, and evolve on your terms.

It was never about being everywhere. It was about being brilliantly effective where it counts. Matching tools to vision. Empowering people. Delighting customers. Delivering value faster than ever.

That mindset, relevance over novelty, became one of the most vital digital disciplines of the time.

And if you look closely, you'll notice that this entire story has a striking resemblance to how AI is shifting the world, as we know it.

Numbers as Narrative (Data)

Data is more than numbers; it's your new business language. Use it to tell stories, drive decisions, and shape strategy.

As digital systems took root in business, something powerful quietly began to surface: data.

At first, many treated data like leftover scraps, buried in dashboards or reports. But those paying close attention saw it differently. Data wasn't just an output. It was fast becoming the most valuable input.

In the early days, data started to guide strategy. Every click, comment, booking, or bounce was a clue. It showed what customers loved, what they skipped, what made them stick, and what sent them packing.

The smartest businesses weren't necessarily the biggest, but they were the sharpest. They used data to fine-tune websites, tweak messages, segment audiences, and lift service. Most importantly, they used it to listen. To really understand their customers, day in and day out.

Airbnb was a standout here. They tracked everything from nights booked, host behaviour, content results, and customer feedback. Their knack for engineering "trust" wasn't guesswork. It was built on seeing what their users actually did.

The real gold was in how intentional it all was. Businesses learned to ask:

- What data do we have?

- What does it actually mean?

- How can it help us serve better?

They also wised up that not all data was equal. Vanity metrics such as likes, impressions, and shares had their place but didn't tell the full story. The shift was toward actionable insights: behaviour, conversions, satisfaction, lifetime value.

Those who did this well treated data with care to build stronger relationships. They used it to build trust, to show customers they were seen, understood, and supported.

7

They also started thinking ethically. With all this power came responsibility. As businesses gained more info on people's preferences, habits, and locations, they had to decide how to use it, or when not to. The smartest brands understood: data wasn't theirs to exploit, it was theirs to honour.

In short, data was power. But like all power, its worth came down to how wisely it was used.

For businesses trying not to drown in data, learning how to harness it became one of the most important skills to master.

And those who made data a living, breathing part of the customer relationship were the ones who unlocked something special: relevance at scale.

Kickstart Execution

Ideas are cheap. Action is priceless. Build momentum by turning vision into value, one smart move at a time

For many businesses stepping into digital back in the 2010s, strategy was often a doc, a slide deck, a roadmap, or a stack of KPIs. It all looked fantastic on paper. But strategy without execution? That's just potential energy.

What we saw in those early years was that real wins rarely came from perfect plans. They came from doing. Rolling up sleeves, testing ideas, falling over, learning fast, and tweaking on the fly.

Digital didn't reward those who moved first. It rewarded those who could move again and again.

Later in this book, we'll see that adopting AI is much the same.

The businesses that soared treated strategy as a living, breathing thing. They tuned in through analytics, customer feedback, and internal chats, using what they learned to keep refining execution.

Execution was about making real, measurable, value-driven progress.

Look at Airbnb again. Their digital game wasn't just clever; it was committed. They set clear goals, built a feedback loop, and constantly tested what worked: which images popped, which platforms converted, which messages landed. They fine-tuned, relentlessly.

The big lesson? Great digital strategies weren't made in silos. They brought marketing, tech, sales, ops, and customer service together into one system that learned, adapted, and grew.

It also meant getting clear on what success meant. Businesses started moving past vanity metrics to indicators that truly mattered: quality leads, happy customers, loyalty, and cost-to-serve.

They realised "likes" and "clicks" were easy to count but hard to cash. So they focused on outcomes: revenue, retention, advocacy, and efficiency.

Team alignment was another massive driver. A digital strategy couldn't live in a corner. It needed champions across the whole business, people who understood the vision, felt ownership, and were ready to act. When digital thinking was shared from the front desk to the C-suite, execution got easier, faster, and more authentic.

And crucially, execution demanded accountability. It wasn't "set and forget." The best businesses built in feedback loops: measuring what mattered, checking in often, and making gutsy calls when something wasn't working.

In that first digital wave, the savviest operators were the most consistent. They knew strategy was a compass, but execution was the actual journey.

And they made sure everyone was walking the same track.

My Journey to Digital Transformation and Beyond

This chapter hasn't looked back just for nostalgia's sake. It's been about uncovering the real roots of transformation. What began as a push to "go digital" by many of the leading businesses sparked a seismic shift in how they think, work, and connect.

This is exactly the journey we all need to take, before stepping into something even bigger: the age of artificial intelligence.

And this brings me back to my own story; the path that brought me here, and why T.H.I.N.K Digital is so personal to me.

My Journey to Digital Transformation and Beyond

It all started in 2002 when I launched a digital transformation agency. Back then, our main gig was helping field service suppliers (tradies, maintenance crews, technicians) get online. We'd build them websites, spruce up their digital profiles, and help them show up where customers were searching.

It was rewarding work that made a real difference for small businesses trying to stand out.

Discovering Deeper Challenges on the Ground

But the more time I spent shoulder-to-shoulder with these clients, the clearer it became that their biggest struggles weren't just about getting found. Once they landed a job, they were drowning in operational headaches: managing compliance paperwork, chasing safety checks, tracking jobs, and sorting invoices.

On top of all that, there was a real disconnect between them and homeowners, who simply wanted things done right.

It was obvious that the market needed more than slick marketing. It needed a complete rethink of how things worked.

A Full Pivot: Building Something the Industry Needed

So we decided to change track completely. We pivoted the agency 360 degrees to create something brand new: a dedicated field service management solution. It wasn't just about helping suppliers win more work - it was about helping them deliver that work better. More efficiently, transparently, and with compliance and safety built in from the start.

Weathering COVID: Finding New Opportunities

Then COVID hit. Practically overnight, the work for many field service suppliers dried up. But even amid all that chaos, we spotted a new opportunity.

We discovered an entirely new audience: Property managers were under pressure to keep essential maintenance ticking along, but they desperately needed suppliers who could guarantee compliance, safety, and fast turnaround during COVID.

That was our moment.

We realised we could actually build an ecosystem that brought everyone together. Suppliers could tap into steady, trusted work; property managers got quality and compliance; owners and occupants had peace of mind. It meant these businesses weren't just chasing random gigs anymore; they were growing sustainably.

Our idea was an instant hit! We secured a landmark deal with one of Australia's biggest Strata Management Groups, helping them connect to a trusted network of compliant suppliers so they could keep properties running smoothly, even during lockdowns.

Rebranding to Scale Globally

That partnership gave us the momentum and proof to take the next leap.

We rebranded as i4T Global, reflecting our vision to take this model beyond Australia and help property managers, suppliers, owners, and tenants work together better all over the world.

Today, i4T Global offers four independent yet fully integrated solutions, delivering a comprehensive PropTech, Field Service Management, and CRM platform. It's designed to support property managers, field service suppliers, and property owners and occupants alike.

A Story That's Still Unfolding

Looking back, I can see how this whole journey was powered by the very ideas we've talked about in this chapter: start with people, use technology with purpose, lean on data for smarter decisions, and stay agile enough to keep evolving.

This isn't just theory for me. It's a road I've walked side by side with the businesses that inspire me every day. And the story is getting even more interesting, as we rewire our business for the AI age.

The mindset is set. The tools are smarter. AI is here, not to replace us, but to boost our thinking, fuel fresh ideas, and drive meaningful growth. The future is wide open for those gutsy enough to THINK forward, and lead with intelligence.

Chapter 2:
AI-first Thinking!

I started as a skeptic first with AI, then, over 12 months of hands-on practice, I realised that Artificial Intelligence is no longer a specialised layer in business; it's becoming the digital core.

In 2025, the companies pulling ahead are the ones that digitised then and are now intelligent by design. What 'AI-first thinking' means for me is placing intelligence at the heart of our business strategies, learning from day-to-day operations, and understanding our own customer experiences.

It means it isn't about replacing people. It's about augmenting people's strengths of speed, creativity, empathy, and decision-making with intelligent systems that work around the clock, learn as we go, and scale without friction.

Whether we are automating workflows, improving our customer support with AI-powered chat, or predicting demand before our competitors do, adopting an AI-first mindset is how we stop reacting and start leading.

What You'll Learn

- What AI-first thinking means (beyond the buzz)

- How to rethink work and value with human-AI collaboration

- Where AI delivers the most return in modern businesses

- How to start embedding intelligence into our existing operations

- Tools, frameworks, and real-world case studies to help us apply it immediately

The Shift From Digital Transformation to AI-First Transformation

The term "digital transformation" has been thrown around so often over the last decade that it's lost most of its weight. By 2025, being "digital" is the baseline, not the goal.

We've shifted from asking "How do we move our business online?" to "How do we make our business smarter, faster, and more adaptive than ever before?" That's where AI-first thinking begins.

What Changed?

A few quiet revolutions converged, and none of them were subtle:

- **Data overflow:** Businesses now generate more data in a day than they used to in a month. But raw data is useless unless you can interpret it in real time. AI became the translator.

- **AI maturity:** What once lived in R&D labs is now available via APIs and plug-and-play platforms. Anyone can embed AI into operations without needing a data science team.

- **Customer expectations:** Instant responses, personalised offers, seamless journeys. Our audience no longer compares us to our industry; they compare us to the last best digital experience we had.

- **Operational demands:** Speed is a survival factor. And while humans can't scale infinitely, AI can, and does, every day.

In short, we no longer need to "Go Digital." We need to Go Intelligent.

AI-First vs. AI-Enabled

Most businesses that we have come across or observed still fall into the trap of treating AI as an enhancement, a way to automate a task or optimise an ad campaign. That's AI-enabled.

An AI-first business sees intelligence as the foundation, not the frosting. It designs processes, customer journeys, and team structures around systems that can predict, learn, and adapt.

AI-Enabled vs AI-First		
	AI-Enabled	**AI-First**
Goal	Efficiency or cost-saving	Strategic Transformation
Impact	Isolated gains	System-wide leverage
Culture	"Let's try it."	"This is how we think and operate."
Use	Patch applied to the existing process	Redesign of the process with intelligence built in

From Static Process to Dynamic Flow

In traditional digital systems, workflows were linear. We followed a certain set of rules. If A happens, do B.

AI-first workflows are non-linear. We can evaluate multiple variables, adjust based on context, and generate their own next best action. This gives businesses what we call adaptive flow: the ability to react and respond like a living organism, not a programmed machine.

Consider the following example.

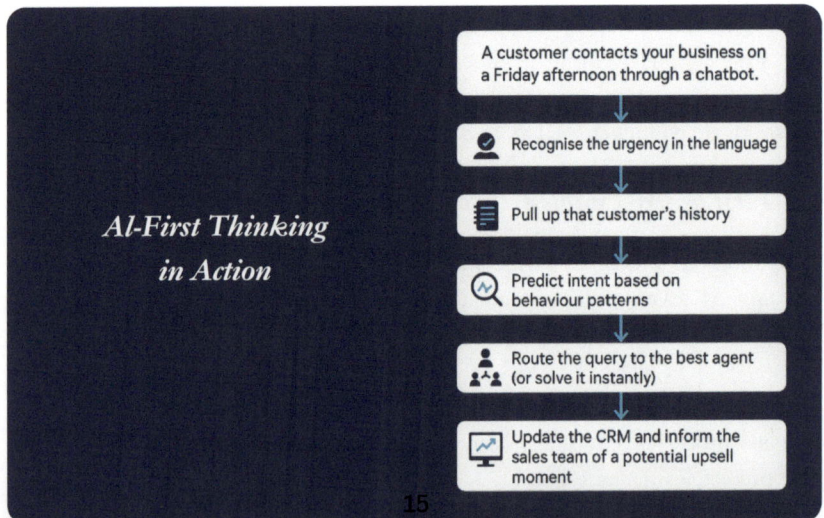

AI-First Thinking in Action

A customer contacts your business on a Friday afternoon through a chatbot.

Recognise the urgency in the language

Pull up that customer's history

Predict intent based on behaviour patterns

Route the query to the best agent (or solve it instantly)

Update the CRM and inform the sales team of a potential upsell moment

No human coded that entire sequence line by line. But it happens seamlessly, because AI connects context, action, and outcome in real time.

The Business Case for Thinking AI-First

We don't need to adopt AI because it's trendy; we adopt it because the alternative is operational drag in many forms.

AI-first thinking isn't about machines doing our work. It's about machines amplifying our work, so we can do more of what matters, better than ever.

Simplifying the Core Concepts

To adopt AI-first thinking, we don't need to be a data scientist or technologist. But we do need to understand what's changing under the hood.

Let's break it down.

What Is AI-First Thinking?

AI-first thinking is the strategic mindset that assumes intelligent systems are not optional add-ons; they are core building blocks of business operations.

It means designing our business's operational workflows, products, and decision-making processes with AI at the centre, not tacked on the side.

It's asking:
- "How can intelligence inform this task?"
- "Where can decisions be predicted, personalised, or automated?"
- "How do we make this process learn as it runs?"

This leads to better outcomes, faster responsiveness, and a more resilient business model.

Did you notice how far we have come from just efficient processes?

The Augmentation Principle

One of the biggest misconceptions about AI is that it replaces humans. In reality, the most effective uses of AI are built around augmentation - amplifying human capabilities, not replacing them.

AI augments:

- Speed: Processing large amounts of data or making decisions in milliseconds
- Focus: Handling repetitive tasks so humans can focus on high-value work
- Insight: Spotting patterns we might miss or can't process at scale
- Consistency: Removing emotional or cognitive bias from routine decisions

Think of AI as your unseen co-pilot, always running in the background, flagging insights, handling grunt work, and learning from every interaction.

Intelligence Embedded Everywhere

AI offers cross-functional capability that can be embedded across nearly every part of a modern business.

Here's where AI-first thinking applies:

AI First Thinking Applications	
Function	Applications
Customer Support	Chatbots, sentiment analysis, query classification
Marketing	Recommendation engines, dynamic creative, content scoring
Sales	Predictive lead scoring, CRM automation
Operations	Demand forecasting, inventory optimisation
HR	Candidate screening, attrition risk analysis
Finance	Fraud detection, cash flow forecasting

You're not building "an AI project." You're embedding intelligence into every function, every decision, every day.

From If-Then Logic to Machine Learning

Traditional digital systems operate on explicit rules:

If A happens, then do B.

AI-first systems use machine learning, which finds patterns in data and adjusts responses over time. That's what allows them to:

- Adapt to new behaviours
- Improve accuracy with more exposure
- Personalise responses based on individual contexts

This transition from hard-coded logic to adaptive learning is what gives AI-first organisations their edge. They don't just scale; they evolve.

18

AI as a Loop, Not a Line

Most traditional workflows are linear. AI-first workflows are looped - they learn, iterate, and improve with each cycle. This feedback loop creates systems that optimise themselves.

AI-POWERED RECOMMENDATION ENGINE

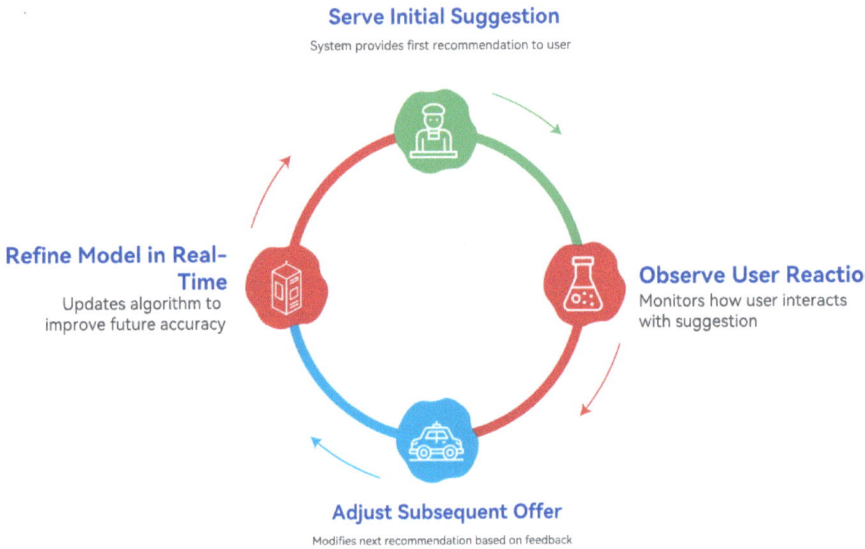

Serve Initial Suggestion

System provides first recommendation to user

Refine Model in Real-Time

Updates algorithm to improve future accuracy

Observe User Reactio

Monitors how user interacts with suggestion

Adjust Subsequent Offer

Modifies next recommendation based on feedback

AI-first thinking isn't about flipping a switch. It's about seeing your business as an ecosystem of intelligence, where every interaction, process, and decision becomes smarter over time.

The Real-World Playbook

Theory is easy to admire. But what makes AI-first thinking real is seeing it work in the wild. The following examples show how forward-thinking companies, both global leaders and homegrown innovators, are putting intelligence at the core of their business models.

At i4T Global, we have already started to implement AI for Strata Managers.

Let's dive into how we, and other market leaders, are tackling some of the biggest industry challenges with AI.

The Challenge

i4T Maintenance - our maintenance management software was approached by strata managers weary of traditional systems that were slow, prone to errors, and relied on manual input, delaying maintenance and frustrating tenants.

The Solution

i4T Maintenance developed its own AI companion, Yara AI, to automatically process tenant requests from SMS or email.

The AI extracts key details (like occupant details and issue descriptions) and creates service requests for strata managers to review.

If anything's unclear, Yara generates a draft for verification, saving time and avoiding errors.

The Outcome

Property managers were now able to deliver an improved tenant experience, making the process easy and efficient for them.

Automated work order processing also ensured quicker issue handling and faster resolutions, while property managers began to save time on admin work and focused more on high-priority tasks.

The Challenge

Canva disrupted the design world by making it easy for anyone to create professional visuals. But as their user base grew into the hundreds of millions, users didn't just want templates, they wanted suggestions, shortcuts, and speed. [3]

The Solution

Canva embedded AI into its very fabric as a layer that amplifies the design process. Users can now:

Auto-generate text with Magic Write (powered by OpenAI)	One-click remove image backgrounds	Instantly translate designs into multiple languages	Get design layout suggestions in real time

The Outcome

Rather than just simplifying design, Canva now accelerates creativity. Users don't realise they're using AI, and that's the point. It feels intuitive, seamless, and helpful.

That's AI-first done right.

▲ ATLASSIAN

The Challenge

As Atlassian scaled tools like Jira and Confluence globally, a key challenge emerged: how to help teams find and act on information faster, especially in large, distributed organisations.[4]

The Solution

Atlassian introduced an AI layer to connect the missing dots.

Confluence document summary
Processes and condenses long documents stored in Confluence into concise summaries

Jira ticket recommendation
Identifies and proposes related tickets and tasks within the Jira platform

Internal query answering
Responds to internal staff questions using natural language input prompts

Content quality monitoring
Detects and alerts on content that is outdated or duplicated across platforms

The Outcome

By embedding AI into knowledge and collaboration workflows, Atlassian turned information overload into focused, actionable insight. Teams now spend less time searching, more time delivering.

Key Pattern Across All Case Studies

These aren't "AI projects." They are AI-powered businesses. What they share is:

- AI integrated into core workflows

- A focus on augmentation, not automation alone

- Continuous learning and iteration from real user behaviour

- Invisible intelligence - the tech serves the experience, not the other way around

AI-first thinking isn't reserved for Silicon Valley or billion-dollar budgets. It's already being done, in Australia, in SMEs, in platforms built for humans by humans, with machines enhancing the work, not replacing it.

Chapter 3:

Hyper-Personalisation in the Age of AI

Today's best-performing businesses don't just use data to market; they use it to understand. They personalise not because the tech is available, but because the customer deserves it.

Some of the big shifts we are witnessing right now are:

- From **segmentation** to **signals**

- From **campaigns** to **conversations**

- From **automation** to **augmentation**

- From **attention** to **authenticity**

This isn't just for tech giants or unicorn startups. Australian brands, from Koala to Vinomofo, are already proving that smart, ethical personalisation can drive growth, loyalty, and impact.

We don't need to personalise everything. We just need to personalise the right things, consistently, respectfully, and intelligently.

From Segmentation to Signals

Not too long ago, if we grouped our customers into a few neat buckets, like age, gender, or postcode, and fired off a few emails tailored to each group, you were considered ahead of the game. That was "personalisation." But let's be honest, most of that was just mass marketing with a sprinkle of data.

Fast forward to 2025, and things have changed. Today's customers can smell 'generic' a mile away. They've been trained by Netflix, Amazon, and Spotify to expect relevance in every interaction, right now, not after the campaign ends.

That means it's time to move beyond segmentation and start listening for signals.

Segmentation is Static. Signals Are Dynamic

Traditional segmentation is like putting our customers into boxes. Helpful at first, but limiting. Signals, on the other hand, are real-time clues that show how someone behaves, what they need, and when they're most likely to act.

Think about it:

- **Segmentation** says: "This customer is a 35-year-old woman in Brisbane."

- **Signals** say: "She just browsed three pages about sustainable packaging, clicked an Instagram ad on compostable mailers, and spent 90 seconds hovering on a pricing table."

Now, which one would you use to tailor a message?

The Pitfalls of Traditional Segmentation

Traditional segmentation doesn't work anymore, due to several reasons:

- Ignores context (what they're doing now)

- Assumes uniformity within groups

- Relies on outdated or irrelevant data

- Treats people like personas, not individuals

In contrast, signal-based personalisation is dynamic, fluid, and adaptive. It reacts to behaviour as it happens, not what was true six months ago.

Behaviour Over Identity

Hyper-personalisation starts when we stop focusing on who someone is and start tuning into *what they're doing*.

Here are a few common signals smart businesses are already using:

- **Scroll depth** on key landing pages

- **Search terms** within our site

- **Cart additions** without checkout

- **Help centre** visits before a purchase

- **Time of day** or device used to browse

These micro-signals, when interpreted well, tell a much richer story than a customer's postcode ever could.

Tools to Help Us Read the Signals

We don't need to be a data scientist to start picking up on behavioural signals. The right tools can do the heavy lifting:

- **Segment**: Unified customer data infrastructure that tracks and organises behaviour across platforms

- **Heap or Mixpanel:** Great for analysing user journeys and behaviours without needing manual tagging

- **Clearbit:** Enriches visitor profiles in real-time so we can match behaviour with business context

These tools act like our business's digital ears, listening, learning, and helping you respond at just the right moment.

Pro Tip
Replace Static Funnels with Dynamic Experience Flows

The old "awareness → interest → decision" funnel assumes people move in straight lines. Reality? They zigzag, loop back, and jump steps. A dynamic experience flow adapts to this behaviour on the fly.

For example:

A potential customer browses our FAQ page → reads a blog on pricing → exits → comes back three days later via mobile → gets a personalised message offering a product comparison and free trial.
That's not a funnel. That's a conversation, powered by signals, not assumptions.

27

From Passive Data to Active Insight

It's one thing to collect data. It's another thing to act on it. Signal-based personalisation doesn't just help you understand your customers, it helps us anticipate them.

The shift is this:

> *Don't just track behaviour. Respond to it. Automatically. Instantly. Personally.*

Because in the age of AI, waiting to personalise after the fact is like checking the weather after your picnic.

The Anatomy of Hyper-Personalisation

Hyper-personalisation isn't a plugin we switch on; it's a layered approach to customer experience. It shows up differently depending on where our customer is in their journey, but the end goal is the same: to make every interaction feel surprisingly relevant, effortlessly helpful, and unmistakably for them.

Here's how that plays out, stage by stage.

Stage 1: Awareness – Tailoring the First Impression

What's happening here:
This is our first hello. Our goal isn't just visibility; it's resonance. Our job is to show potential customers that we get them before they even realise what they need.

This is where the customer journey begins, often invisibly.

A click on a Google search. A scroll past an Instagram ad. A visit to our website at 10:48 pm from a mobile device. It's the moment we go from unknown to noticed.

In the past, this stage relied heavily on broad targeting: shouting our message to as many people as possible and hoping it landed. But in today's landscape, attention is scarce, and relevance is everything.

Hyper-personalisation at this stage means crafting messages that resonate immediately, based on live signals and context. It's about making someone feel like they've landed in the right place, at the right time, with a brand that already speaks their language, before they've even introduced themselves.

This is where we create our first emotional hook. If it feels right, they'll stay. If it feels generic, they'll bounce.

Stage 2: Consideration – Guiding Smart Decision-Making

What's happening here:
The customer is now exploring. They've shown interest; our job is to guide them, not with a sales push, but with content, comparisons, and recommendations that speak to where they are, not just who they are.

Once we've made a strong first impression, our potential customer moves into the consideration stage. Here, they're weighing their options. They're comparing us to others. They're exploring, questioning, and asking (consciously or not):

"Is this brand right for me?"

In traditional marketing, this stage relied on generic nurture sequences, product comparison tables, and maybe a webinar invite. But in the age of AI, customers expect more. They expect us to know what they care about, which pain points they've expressed (even through clicks and scrolls), and what information they need next.

Hyper-personalisation here is all about supporting the decision-making process without overwhelming or hard-selling. It's like being a helpful guide rather than a pushy salesperson, using data and behavioural cues to offer relevant insights, content, and proof at the right moment.

At this stage, trust is built through relevance. We need to show that we understand their unique journey, and they'll stay longer. Maybe for life.

Stage 3: Conversion – Removing Friction with Relevance

What's happening here:
This is decision time. We've got their interest. Now make saying "yes" as easy and personalised as possible. Anticipate objections. Surface the right features, the right price, the right nudge at the right moment.

This is the tipping point, where interest turns into intent, and intent (hopefully) becomes action.

The conversion stage is where so many businesses lose the customer. Not because we don't offer a great product, but because the final stretch feels clunky, generic, or confusing. Decision fatigue, pricing doubt, or the absence of tailored reassurance can cause someone to walk away, sometimes seconds from clicking "buy."

Hyper-personalisation here is our secret weapon. It removes friction by replacing guesswork with guidance. It creates confidence by offering the right message, incentive, or support based on the person's unique path up to this point.

Whether it's a personalised offer, a smart chatbot nudge, or a custom product bundle based on their cart contents, personalisation at this stage doesn't push. It clears the way. Done right, it feels less like selling and more like helping someone make a decision they were ready for.

Stage 4: Post-Purchase & Loyalty – Keeping it Personal After the Sale

What's happening here:
This is decision time. We've got their interest. Now make saying "yes" as easy and personalised as possible. Anticipate objections. Surface the right features, the right price, the right nudge at the right moment.

Too many businesses treat the sale as the finish line. In reality, it's only the beginning.

In this stage, our customer is no longer deciding whether to trust us; they already have. Now the question becomes:

"Was it worth it?"
"Would I do it again?"
"Do they still care about me, or just my money?"

Hyper-personalisation in post-purchase is about deepening the relationship. It's our chance to follow through on our promise, anticipate next steps, and continue delivering value in a way that feels tailor-made.

This might look like personalised onboarding, thoughtful follow-up content, loyalty rewards based on real behaviour, or even perfectly timed reorder nudges. And crucially, it's about remembering who they are, not just treating them like another transaction.

Get this stage right, and we don't just earn a repeat customer. We create an advocate.

How AI Powers the Shift

In the early days of digital marketing, personalisation was manual, time-consuming, hard to scale, and often reliant on assumptions. We'd create segments, write different email versions, and test landing pages. It helped, but it only scratched the surface.

Now, with AI, we've entered a new era: real-time, context-aware, behaviour-driven personalisation, at scale.

But how does AI do that?

Let's break it down into practical parts.

Machine Learning vs Manual Logic
The traditional approach was something like this:

"If customer clicks Product A → send Email B."
Linear. Predictable. Static.

AI Approach:

Machine learning models detect patterns across thousands of behaviours; clicks, scrolls, hesitations, purchases, and learn what nudges move the needle.

For example:

- A human might say: "People who buy shampoo are likely to buy conditioner."

- AI discovers: "People who buy shampoo after 10 pm and read a blog post on 'hair thinning' are more likely to buy the scalp serum instead."

That's the difference. AI doesn't just follow logic. It learns logic from live behaviour, and adapts every day.

AI Doesn't Just Automate, it Adapts in Real Time

Most automation systems are reactive. They wait for inputs, then follow preset instructions.

AI-powered personalisation is proactive. It:

- Predicts what the user might do next

- Personalises the next step without needing pre-coded rules

- Continuously refines itself as new data comes in

For example:

- A first-time visitor gets a welcome message tailored to their device, time of day, and referral source.

- If they return via email but hesitate at checkout, the AI shifts the messaging, perhaps offering a product comparison or reviews from similar users.

This is what we call adaptive experience flow. It's less like a funnel and more like a conversation. Soon, our customers will begin to see us as responsive, fluid, and smart.

AI Unlocks Hyper-Personalisation at Scale

Without AI, personalisation breaks under pressure. We simply can't:

- Write 200+ versions of our welcome email

- Tailor product recommendations for every user by hand

- Predict customer churn patterns in real time

- Monitor millions of behavioural signals simultaneously

AI does this effortlessly, not by replacing human creativity, but by scaling human insight. It's like giving our best marketing brain an army of assistants that work 24/7, never sleep, and learn faster than we can blink.

"In the old world, we hoped our message landed. In the AI world, we know it did, and we're already optimising the next one."

Micro-Moments Are the New Battleground

Google coined the term micro-moments: those fleeting points in time when a user wants to know something, go somewhere, do something, or buy now. [5] These moments are windows of opportunity, and they vanish fast.

AI helps us:
- Recognise them in real time (e.g., "user just switched from browsing to comparing")

- React with precision (e.g., surface a product demo or offer a side-by-side comparison)

- Trigger the next best action based on live intent

This is where AI shines: it compresses decision-making into seconds. The right content, to the right person, at the right time, without anyone needing to lift a finger.

The Basics of Micro-Moments

Want to develop a strategy to shape your consumer's decisions?
Start by understanding the key micro-moments in their journey.

micro-moment | mīkrō-mōmənt

NOUN
An intent-rich moment when a person turns to
a device to act on a need—to know, go, do, or buy.

There are 4 game-changing moments that really matter.

I-want-to-know moments:	I-want-to-go moments:	I-want-to-do moments:	I-want-to-buy moments:
When someone is exploring or researching, but is not necessarily in purchase mode.	When someone is looking for a local business or is considering buying a product at a nearby store.	When someone wants help completing a task or trying something new.	When someone is ready to make a purchase and may need help deciding what to buy or how to buy it.

In these moments, consumers want what they want, when they
want it—and they're drawn to brands that **deliver on their needs**.

Be there:
Anticipate the
micro-moments for your
target audience, and commit
to being there to help when
those moments occur.

Be useful:
Provide a digital
experience that's relevant
to consumers' needs in the
moment, and quickly
connect people to the
answers they're looking for.

Be accountable:
Create a seamless
customer experience across
all screens and channels,
and measure the collective
impact across them, too.

34

AI Connects the Dots Across Platforms

Our customers don't think in channels. They browse on mobile, chat via social, click through email, and buy on desktop, all within 48 hours.

AI-powered solutions (like customer data platforms and cross-channel orchestration tools) unify that fragmented behaviour into a single journey.

That means:

- The blog post they read on Monday influences the email they get on Tuesday

- Their product search in your app affects what shows up on the homepage on Friday

- The support question they asked last week informs the loyalty offer you serve today

AI isn't just a feature anymore. It's the nervous system connecting our entire customer experience.

AI Capabilities Overview

Pattern Recognition
Know what works, before your competition does

Predictive Analytics
Anticipate churn, intent, or lifetime value and act early

Personalisation Engines
Dynamically adapt your website, ads, and emails based on user context

Real-time Decisioning
Deliver the right message in the moment, not hours later

Language Generation
Write custom content, emails, or product descriptions at scale

"Do I Need a Data Scientist to Use This?"

Nope. Most modern AI tools are designed for marketers, founders, and operators, not engineers.

Today's platforms bring AI to the frontlines, without the jargon or code.

AI makes hyper-personalisation not only possible, but practical, for SMEs, scaleups, and even solo entrepreneurs.

It transforms marketing from scheduled to situational, sales from funnels to fluid flows, support from responsive to anticipatory, and loyalty from points to personal connections.

And the best part? Once AI is trained, it never sleeps. It learns while we rest. It improves while we grow.

Privacy, Trust, and the New Value Exchange

Personalisation is powerful. But with great power comes… consent.

In a world where AI can predict our next move before we even make it, the question turns from "what we personalise" to "how we do it".

It all starts with trust.

Hyper-personalisation works because it feels relevant. But push it too far, or do it without permission, and it crosses the line from helpful to creepy. One wrong move, and our brand stops feeling personal and starts feeling invasive.

That's why in 2025, data ethics and transparency aren't just legal requirements, they're strategic differentiators.

The Trust Shift: From Data Collection to Data Collaboration

Gone are the days when businesses could quietly track behaviour in the background and stitch together profiles without consent. Customers are more informed, more empowered, and more protective of their data than ever.

What they want now is a value exchange.

"If I give you my data, what do I get in return?"
"Can I trust you to use it wisely, and only with my permission?"
Smart businesses know how to earn data through transparency, choice, and value.

Types of Data and What They Mean for Personalisation

Understanding how data is shared (or not) is critical to earning and keeping trust.

Type	What It Is	Who Owns It	Personalisation Use
Zero-party data	Info customers *intentionally* share (e.g., quizzes, preferences, surveys)	Customer	Most trusted and powerful
First-party data	Data from our own platforms (e.g., website visits, purchases)	We	Essential for real-time personalisation
Second-party data	Someone else's first-party data shared via a partnership	Partnered Brand	Use with caution and consent
Third-party data	Purchased or scraped from external sources	Aggregators	Becoming obsolete and untrusted

Pro tip: Build a strategy around zero- and first-party data. It's clean, consented, and far more accurate than bought lists or stitched profiles.

Building Trust: The 4 Principles of Ethical Personalisation

Personalisation without trust is manipulation. These four principles ensure our approach is not only effective but also ethically grounded and customer-approved.

1. Transparency

- Tell users exactly what we are collecting and why.

- Use plain English, not legalese.

- Show, don't hide, data policies in emails, apps, and sites.

2. Control

- Give people a preference centre to manage what they receive.

- Let them update interests, communication channels, and frequency.

3. Value

- Make the personalisation worth it.

- If someone gives you their birthday, send more than a "Happy Birthday" email. Surprise them with a relevant reward or personalised experience.

4. Security

- Keep data safe.

- Make it clear that you use trusted platforms, comply with global privacy laws (GDPR, CCPA), and prioritise encryption and access control.

Where Personalisation Crosses the Line

If a customer ever says, "Wait, how do you know that?", we've likely gone too far. Watch for these red flags:

- Recommending a product someone mentioned once in a private chat

- Using behavioural data without permission (e.g., tracking every mouse move)

- Serving ads based on something a user typed in a support form

Personalisation without permission is no longer clever. It's clumsy. And it erodes trust faster than any broken link.

The New Loyalty: Built on Consent, Not Cookies

With third-party cookies disappearing and data laws tightening, the future of personalisation belongs to brands that prioritise:

- Opt-in experiences

- Real relationships

- And customer empowerment

In return, we don't just get clicks. We get loyalty. The kind that lasts beyond campaigns and builds brand equity with every respectful interaction.

Hyper-personalisation isn't just about what we can do; it's about what we should do.

When we ask clearly, respect boundaries, and deliver real value, customers want to share their data. And that's when personalisation becomes sustainable.

THE HYPER-PERSONALISATION TOOLKIT

Start small. Move smart. Scale fast.

Hyper-personalisation doesn't need a massive tech stack or team; just the right mindset and a few clever moves. Here's a simplified 4-step framework to get started today.

AUDIT YOUR JOURNEY

Find the friction. Where do all customers see the same thing, regardless of their behaviour or context?

Tool to try: Hotjar for behaviour heatmaps

MAP THE SIGNALS

Identify what data you already have: page visits, purchase history, quiz responses, email opens.

Tool to try: Segment or Zapier to unify and connect your platforms

OPTIMISE ONE FLOW

Choose a high-impact touchpoint, like welcome email or cart abandonment, and personalise just one part.

Tool to try: Klaviyo or Mailchimp with conditional logic

BUILD IT INTO RHYTHM

Review weekly what's working. Run one small personalisation test each month. Log wins and double down.

Tool to try: Notion or a shared doc to track and tweak experiments

BONUS TIP: USE AI TO ACCELERATE

Ask ChatGPT or Jasper to draft personalised messages based on behaviour. Then we refine it with our brand voice.

Prompt example: "Write a friendly follow-up email for someone who viewed Product X twice but didn't buy."

The Real-World Playbook

What makes AI-first thinking real is seeing it work in the wild. The following examples show how forward-thinking companies are putting personalisation at the core of their business models.

Koala – Personalised Product Discovery Without the Push

 ## The Challenge

With a growing product range and a fiercely competitive e-commerce space, Koala needed a way to guide customers to the right product without friction. [6]

 ## The Solution

Koala launched an on-site product quiz asking about sleeping style, firmness preference, and budget. Based on real-time responses, the site dynamically served the best-fit mattress, matching headlines and images to the user's answers.

 ## The Outcome

Higher engagement, reduced return rates, and a more "human" shopping experience, all powered by zero-party data and clever logic.

✛HealthMatch

HealthMatch – Smart Personalisation for Serious Decisions

The Challenge

As a platform matching patients to clinical trials, HealthMatch needed to personalise not just for convenience, but for trust. [7]

The Solution

AI was used to assess eligibility criteria and tailor trial suggestions based on a user's health data, location, and urgency, all while maintaining strict privacy and opt-in consent.

The Outcome

Patients received faster matches. Trust grew through transparency. And the platform scaled without sacrificing personal care.

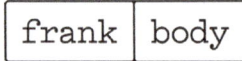

Frank Body – Loyalty Through Relevance

The Challenge

With a cult following and a crowded skincare market, Frank Body needed to retain and re-engage customers more meaningfully. [8]

The Solution

Customers could update preferences, skin type, routine, and concerns, which fed into email flows, product recommendations, and loyalty rewards. Campaigns were triggered by timing (e.g., post-purchase windows) and behaviour (e.g., product page visits without a buy).

The Outcome

Engagement lifted. Reviews spiked. Customers felt like the brand knew them, not just their skin type, but their vibe.

Chapter 4:

No-Code / Low-Code Empowerment for Teams

Not too long ago, if we had an idea for improving a customer journey, streamlining a process, or launching a new campaign, there were only two ways forward: join the back of the dev queue… or give up.

That's changed.

Thanks to the rise of no-code and low-code platforms, everyday team members, marketers, ops leads, and customer service pros are building tools, automating workflows, and launching digital experiences without writing a single line of code. What spreadsheets did for finance, no-code is doing for business builders.

This is the rise of the citizen creator [9], where innovation is no longer limited by technical skill, but fuelled by proximity to the problem.

From launching dynamic landing pages to automating internal handoffs, from building personalised quizzes to spinning up lightweight CRMs, today's best teams don't wait for tech. They build it themselves.

In 2025, digital transformation isn't a department. It's a mindset, shared by every team member who sees something broken and dares to fix it.

This chapter explores how no-code and low-code tools are helping SMEs, startups, and even corporate teams move faster, test smarter, and empower their people to build what they once only dreamed of.

What Is No-Code / Low-Code?

No-code and low-code platforms are exactly what they sound like: ways to build digital tools and automate processes without writing code (or with very minimal help from it).

But this isn't a tech shortcut. It's a business game-changer.

No-Code:

Think drag-and-drop. Think visual builders. These tools let anyone, not just developers, create:

- Websites

- Apps

- Forms

- Workflows

- Dashboards

...using simple interfaces and logic blocks, no technical background required.

Examples:
- A marketer creates a landing page in Webflow

- A customer service rep sets up a feedback form in Typeform

- An ops manager automates an onboarding workflow in Zapier

Low-Code:

This is the middle ground. We still get the visual tools, but with some light coding flexibility when needed. This is ideal for slightly more complex builds or custom integrations.

Examples:
- A startup founder uses Glide to build a mobile client portal

- A small agency connects multiple CRMs using Make.com and custom webhooks

Why This Matters Now

In the early days of digital transformation, everything had to be custom-built, from websites, CRMs, forms, and automations. That meant delays, developer backlogs, and high costs.

Moving beyond 2025, the biggest business advantage isn't who can build the most complex solution. It's who can build the fastest, test quickly, and adapt on the fly.

That's what no-code enables:

- A/B testing a new sales funnel by Tuesday

- Launching a new internal tool without submitting an IT ticket

- Personalising a customer journey because you spotted a friction point, not six months after a strategy review

The tools are ready. The use cases are endless. And the barriers are gone.

What used to take months of planning and expensive development now takes hours, with the right platform, the right mindset, and a willingness to experiment.

The Business Case for Empowerment

Giving our team the tools to build might be the smartest move we made this year. Earlier this year, the operations manager at i4T Global, noticed that the employee onboarding process was slow. It often required a week of manual work from multiple departments to create accounts, assign system access, and generate Jira tickets.

With a low-code/no-code solution, we automated this process with a single email that triggers the creation of accounts, system access, and Jira tickets; tasks that would typically take hours now happen in minutes. What once required a dedicated person and days of work is now streamlined, allowing us to focus on more strategic tasks while dramatically improving efficiency.

That's what no-code is unlocking today.

When we talk about no-code/low-code, we're not just talking about tools. We're talking about team empowerment; the ability for non-technical staff to act on ideas, fix problems, and test new solutions without waiting for technical permission.

Let's unpack the core benefits:

Speed: From Idea to Action in Hours, Not Weeks

Every business has ideas on the whiteboard that never get built. Why? Because time is limited, developers are stretched, and priorities shift.

No-code eliminates that bottleneck. It gives the power to do fast and stay competitive.

Cost-Effective: More Building, Less Budget Burn

Hiring developers or outsourcing even small builds can rack up thousands. Worse, delays mean opportunity costs, the revenue you didn't earn because the fix took too long.

No-code tools shift that balance:

- Monthly platform fees instead of project-based dev hours

- Internal staff solving problems directly

- Less time managing tech = more time delivering value

Agility: Rapid Testing, Learning, and Iteration

The digital landscape doesn't wait. Consumer behaviours shift, platforms update, and competitors adapt.

No-code lets us try something now, get feedback, and adjust instantly. We're no longer trapped in quarterly release cycles or decision paralysis.

No-code gives us the freedom to experiment and the confidence to move fast.

Cross-Team Collaboration Becomes Natural

No-code tools are built for collaboration. They're visual, intuitive, and easy to share. Marketers can hand off working forms to designers. Ops can co-build a process with finance. Sales and support can design tools together.

Suddenly, digital problem-solving stops being an IT activity and becomes a shared business goal.

Empowers the People Closest to the Problem to Solve It

Here's the truth: our developers probably don't use our CRM, marketing workflows, or internal handover tools. But our marketers, customer support reps, and ops team do, every single day.

They know where the pain is. They know what's missing.

When we give those team members the ability to build their own solutions, we boost morale, remove dependencies, and unlock innovation.

What No-Code/Low-Code Unlocks for Your Business

Speed Advantage
Faster launch and real-time action

Operational Agility
Quick testing, tweaking, scaling

Staff Empowerment
Transforms staff into creators

Cost Efficiency
Reduces development and agency costs

Innovation Driver
User-centric solution development

Where No-Code Shines Across the Business

The beauty of no-code and low-code platforms is their flexibility. They're not just for marketing. They solve real operational headaches across our entire organisation, from internal team workflows to customer-facing experiences.

Let's look at how different departments are using these tools to simplify, automate, and transform the way they work, without needing IT or technical expertise.

Turn Marketing Ideas into Experiences

Marketing is often where no-code gets its biggest applause, and for good reason. Marketers thrive on speed and iteration, but are often bottlenecked by tech requests. With no-code tools, they can create landing pages, build forms, trigger automations, and personalise customer journeys without writing a single line of code.

And it's not just speed; it's relevance.

With smart forms, quizzes, and triggers, marketers can tailor messaging to each user based on behaviour, preferences, or referral source; the kind of personalisation that used to take weeks of dev time.

Automate Mundane Operations

Operations is the backbone of any business, but it's often bogged down with repetitive tasks, disconnected systems, and manual reporting. No-code changes that. It allows ops teams to automate workflows and create internal tools that keep the wheels turning, without spreadsheets and sticky notes.

With no-code tools, they can build apps and dashboards that look great, work smoothly, and eliminate hours of admin every week.

The big win? Empowering ops staff to design their own solutions, instead of relying on IT to fix problems they experience daily.

Speed Up Service Without Sacrificing Personal Touch

Sales and support teams live and die by response time and context. No-code tools help these teams automate common tasks, streamline data handling, and give reps access to better information instantly.

In customer service, a rep could create a simple ticketing system that tracks unresolved issues and automatically pings follow-up reminders. Or build a feedback loop where customer responses trigger different support flows depending on sentiment. Happy customers are asked for reviews, and frustrated ones are escalated immediately.

Sales and support don't want more systems. They want fewer clicks and smarter handoffs. No-code delivers exactly that.

Prototyping Products Without Engineering

For teams responsible for developing new ideas from product features to new services, no-code platforms offer a way to test fast and fail cheaply.

We can also gather user feedback with live forms, conduct early sign-up interest with embedded waitlists, or build internal beta tester dashboards to manage test rollouts.

In essence, no-code removes the technical hurdle between idea and validation, which is priceless in the early stages of innovation.

Streamline HR and Employee Engagement

HR and people ops are often overloaded with manual tasks such as onboarding, leave requests, compliance docs, and training checklists. No-code lets HR teams take control of these processes and build smooth, self-serve systems that reduce admin while improving employee experience.

HR teams can also use no-code tools for onboarding or to create anonymous feedback channels, internal comms hubs, or performance tracking dashboards. They get to own the employee experience without depending on IT for every change.

Every team in a business has its challenges. No-code doesn't just offer one solution; it offers a way for each department to design its own tools, fix its own gaps, and move with speed and confidence.

The question isn't "Where can no-code help?"

It's "What are we still doing manually that our team could build a better way for, today?"

5 Steps to Making No-Code Work Culture-Wide

No-code only delivers impact when it becomes part of our team's daily rhythm, not just a side project or something "the tech-savvy ones do."

Here's how to embed no-code thinking across our businesses:

1. Start with One Team, One Problem

Pick a real pain point, like onboarding, reporting, or lead capture, and invite one team to solve it using no-code tools. Keep it small. Keep it practical.

2. Upskill with Light, Hands-On Training

Run a 60-minute "build session" or lunch-and-learn. Use templates. Keep it non-technical. The goal isn't to make developers; it's to build confidence.

3. Nominate No-Code Champions

Every department has someone who loves tinkering. Empower them to lead experiments and help others. They'll become our team's internal innovation engine.

4. Create a Shared Toolkit

Make a Notion page or shared doc with tools, tutorials, and internal templates. Celebrate small wins to build momentum.

5. Keep it Safe, Not Restrictive

Set light guardrails like data privacy, naming conventions, and platform approvals, so creativity thrives without chaos.

When our people feel trusted to build, they'll stop asking permission and start solving real problems.

Common Pitfalls

Giving our team the power to build is exciting. But without a little structure, it can lead to confusion, wasted time, or even security risks.

Here are the most common missteps, and how to avoid them.

1. Chaos Without Structure

Letting everyone build without coordination can lead to messy, overlapping systems. We can avoid this by creating shared naming conventions, workflows, and a central place to document what's been built and why.

2. Shadow IT

Teams using tools without visibility from leadership or IT can expose the business to data and compliance risks. We can avoid it by encouraging openness. Give teams freedom to build, but keep a simple approval and integration checklist.

3. Data Silos

When different teams build their own tools with no integration, insights and efficiency suffer. We can avoid this by linking key tools to a central system and reviewing data flows monthly.

4. Overbuilding Too Soon

Trying to automate everything at once leads to complexity and confusion. We can avoid this by starting with one high-impact use case. Get it working. Then scale what succeeds.

5. No Exit Plan

Sometimes a no-code solution outgrows its usefulness, but no one plans for what's next. We can avoid this by regularly reviewing what's been built. When something becomes mission-critical, consider transitioning to a more robust system.

No-Code Common Pitfalls

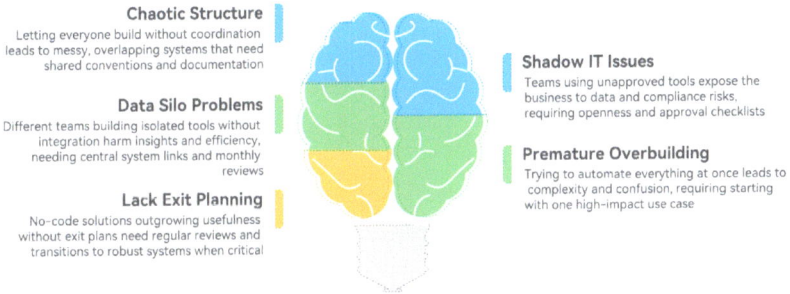

Chaotic Structure
Letting everyone build without coordination leads to messy, overlapping systems that need shared conventions and documentation

Data Silo Problems
Different teams building isolated tools without integration harm insights and efficiency, needing central system links and monthly reviews

Lack Exit Planning
No-code solutions outgrowing usefulness without exit plans need regular reviews and transitions to robust systems when critical

Shadow IT Issues
Teams using unapproved tools expose the business to data and compliance risks, requiring openness and approval checklists

Premature Overbuilding
Trying to automate everything at once leads to complexity and confusion, requiring starting with one high-impact use case

Power to the People

In a world where change moves faster than roadmaps, the true edge isn't just having the right tools, it's having the right people empowered to use them.

No-code and low-code platforms have opened the gates. Our teams no longer need to wait for developers, budget cycles, or external approvals. If they see a problem, they can build the solution, quickly, affordably, and intelligently.

This chapter wasn't just about saving time or cutting costs. It's about showing small businesses how to create a culture of doers. People who fix problems and build systems, rather than reporting problems and getting stuck in the cracks.

And in the age of AI, that kind of agility isn't just helpful. It's non-negotiable.

Chapter 5:

Agentic Systems: The Rise of Autonomous Workflows

We're living in a world where technology isn't just a tool we use; it's beginning to think for us, act on its own, and run entire workflows with minimal human input. This is the rise of agentic systems: AI-driven processes that don't just automate tasks; they learn, adapt, and make decisions on their own.

Today, businesses aren't just using AI to automate menial tasks or optimise customer service responses. They're empowering AI to run workflows autonomously, making decisions, adjusting processes, and continuously improving itself in real-time.

While automation was about replacing repetitive work, agentic systems take things a step further. They are designed to be intelligent, scalable, and proactive. They don't wait for someone to tell them what to do next. Instead, they analyse data, predict outcomes, and act, often without human intervention.

Think about our daily operations: Sales processes, customer support, and inventory management. In many businesses today, these workflows are still run by humans, albeit assisted by automation. But what if we didn't have to manage these tasks at all? What if AI could not only assist, but also autonomously handle the heavy lifting?

In this chapter, we explore how agentic systems are transforming business workflows, from customer service chatbots to self-managing inventory systems. We'll look at how these systems are built, how they evolve, and most importantly, how we can start implementing them in our own business to improve efficiency, scalability, and agility.

> The future of work isn't just humans and machines working side by side. It's machines that think, learn, and act on their own, allowing humans to focus on what truly matters.

What Are Agentic Systems?

AI that doesn't just assist, but acts autonomously.

At its core, an agentic system is an AI-driven system that doesn't simply follow a set of pre-programmed rules; it makes decisions, learns from data, and adapts to new situations on its own.

These systems can act autonomously, which means they can run processes from start to finish, without constant human oversight.

Breaking Down the Basics: Automation vs. Agentic Systems

We all have heard of **automation** before; it's been a buzzword for years. Automation takes repetitive, rule-based tasks and runs them with minimal human input. We can set a rule like, "If a customer's purchase is over $100, send a thank-you email," and the system will do it every time.

Agentic systems, however, take it a step further. They don't just follow rules; they learn and adapt to changing circumstances. They're designed to make intelligent decisions based on real-time data, adjust to new inputs, and improve over time without needing human intervention.

Feature	Automation	Agentic Systems
Definition	Executes repetitive tasks based on predefined rules.	Makes decisions, learns, and adapts based on real-time data.
Flexibility	Fixed rules and processes, no change without human intervention.	Dynamic, adapts to new data and changing conditions.
Learning Ability	Does not learn or adapt. It follows a set script or rule.	Learns over time, improves decisions based on new inputs and feedback.
Decision-Making	Follows predetermined logic (e.g., if this, then that).	Makes intelligent decisions based on patterns and data analysis.
Data Handling	Executes tasks with limited data (often one-step triggers).	Processes large volumes of data and makes predictions based on them.

Real-Time Adaptation	Operates based on static inputs and doesn't adjust unless reprogrammed.	Responds in real-time to changes in data or customer behaviour.
Human Involvement	Minimal to no human input once set up.	Requires oversight but acts with autonomy in its given scope.
Use Case Examples	Sending automated emails, updating CRM records.	AI-driven chatbots that handle customer inquiries, predictive lead scoring.
Scale of Use	Best for repeating high-volume, simple tasks.	Ideal for complex, decision-heavy workflows that require adaptation.
Adaptability to New Situations	Limited adaptability — must be manually reprogrammed for new conditions.	Can automatically adjust to new circumstances and learn from them.

How Agentic Systems Work

At a high level, agentic systems are built on machine learning, real-time data processing, and feedback loops. Here's how it works:

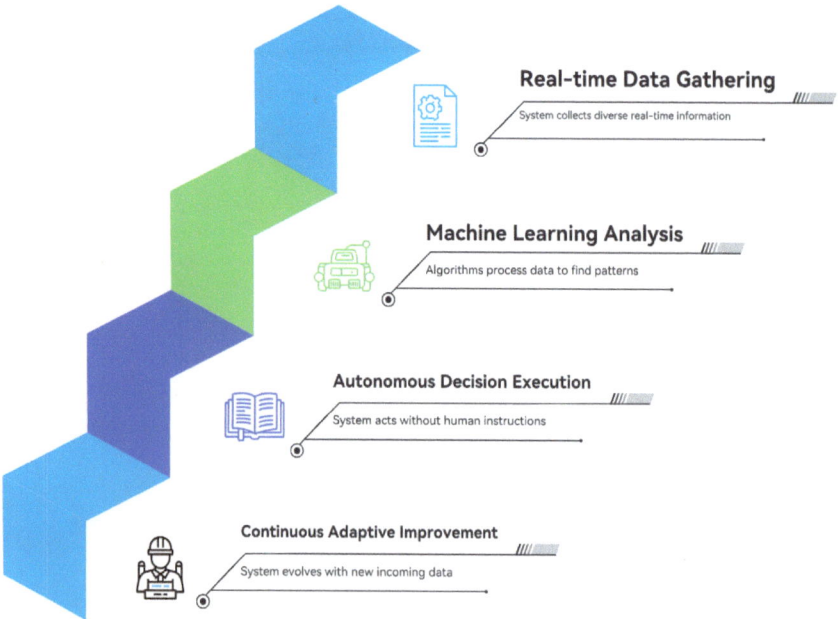

Real-time Data Gathering
System collects diverse real-time information

Machine Learning Analysis
Algorithms process data to find patterns

Autonomous Decision Execution
System acts without human instructions

Continuous Adaptive Improvement
System evolves with new incoming data

AI that Thinks and Acts on Its Own

The key to understanding agentic systems is to think of them as intelligent agents working within our business.

These agents aren't just following a script; they're using data to make decisions, adjusting their actions as they learn, and automating processes that would otherwise require constant supervision.

Take a self-managing inventory system, for example:

- An agentic system continuously monitors stock levels, predicts future demand based on historical sales data, and automatically adjusts orders with suppliers.

- If demand suddenly spikes for a particular product, the system adapts, ordering more stock, alerting the team, and even adjusting pricing in real time.

In this case, we have created a process that runs autonomously and scales efficiently without needing someone to manage it day-to-day.

From Task Automation to Intelligent Decision Making

While traditional automation systems are like a set of instructions that repeat based on fixed inputs, agentic systems are much more dynamic. They evolve as they receive new data, make decisions based on real-time inputs, and adapt their actions in response.

Consider an AI-powered system that tracks leads in a CRM. An automation system might simply send an email after a lead reaches a certain stage. But an agentic system will evaluate the lead's behaviour (e.g., which emails they clicked, what content they read) and send a tailored message, prioritise certain leads, and suggest the next best actions for the sales team. It continuously learns from customer behaviour and adjusts its outreach accordingly.

Why Agentic Systems Matter for Your Business

These systems aren't just a way to automate tasks; they're about creating an agile, adaptable business that can evolve and scale without additional resources.

With the rise of agentic systems, businesses experience a multitude of benefits, including:

1. Increased Efficiency

AI handles repetitive tasks without human input, freeing up time for your team to focus on high-value work.

2. Scalability

Autonomous systems scale effortlessly; no need for additional staff as your business grows.

3. Smarter Decision-Making

AI uses data to make real-time, accurate decisions that improve over time, helping you make informed choices faster.

4. Speed

Instant decisions and actions, cutting down response times and improving customer satisfaction.

5. Consistency

Every decision is made according to preset rules, ensuring uniformity and reliability in operations.

6. Enhanced Customer Experience

Personalised, proactive engagement at scale; customers get the right experience at the right time.

7. Cost Efficiency

Automating complex workflows reduces the need for extra resources, making operations leaner and more cost-effective.

8. Improved Agility

Adapt to market changes in real-time with AI that adjusts to new data and conditions, keeping your business agile.

Benefits of Autonomy in Business

Cost Efficiency
Automating complex workflows cuts extra resource needs, making operations leaner

Improved Agility
AI adjusts to new data and conditions, helping business adapt to market changes instantly

Operational Consistency
Every decision uses preset rules ensuring uniformity and reliability in operations

Better Customer Experience
Personalised, proactive engagement at scale delivers right experience at right time

Smarter Decisions
AI uses data to make real-time, accurate decisions improving over time for informed choices

Faster Speed
Instant decisions and actions reduce response times, enhancing customer satisfaction

Increased Efficiency
AI handles repetitive tasks without human input, freeing team time for high-value work

Enhanced Scalability
Autonomous systems scale effortlessly; no need for additional staff as business grows

How Agentic Systems Are Built

At its core, an agentic system is more than just an automation tool. It's like handing our business an intelligent assistant, one that doesn't just follow commands, but learns from the data, adapts to new conditions, and takes action based on real-time insights.

Key Components of Agentic Systems

Agentic systems aren't some futuristic sci-fi idea. They're built on a few powerful ingredients that work together to make them smart, agile, and capable of managing complex tasks on their own.

Here's how it works:

1. Machine Learning

Machine learning (ML) is what gives agentic systems the ability to think, learn, and adapt. It's like teaching our system how to get better at something over time, just like a human would.

- Supervised Learning: Think of this as a "learning by example" approach. The system gets labelled data (e.g., images of dogs and cats) and learns to recognise patterns (dog = fur, cat = whiskers). Over time, it can apply what it's learned to make predictions.

- Unsupervised Learning: This one's a bit like a detective. The system looks at the data, finds hidden patterns, and figures out what's important, all without human guidance. It's great for customer segmentation or spotting trends.

- Reinforcement Learning: Here's where the system learns by trial and error. It takes actions, gets rewarded (or not), and learns the best way to act next. It's how AI agents get smarter with every decision.

2. Real-Time Data Processing

For an agentic system to make the right decision, it needs real-time data.

The system gathers data from different sources, like customer interactions, sales data, web traffic, or inventory levels, and processes it on the spot. This gives the AI the context it needs to make decisions that feel relevant in the moment.

3. Feedback Loops & Continuous Learning

Agentic systems don't stop learning. They improve continuously, based on new data, feedback, and outcomes.

- Data Feedback: As more data flows in, the system tweaks its decision-making. For example, a chatbot might start with basic responses, but over time, it learns from customer interactions and gets better at solving problems.

- User Feedback: For systems like AI-driven customer support, user ratings or satisfaction surveys help the system adjust its responses. The more interactions it has, the more accurate it becomes.

How Agentic Systems Use Data

Data is the fuel that powers agentic systems. But how does it actually work? Let's break it down:

1. Data Collection

Agentic systems start by collecting data, and the more diverse the data, the better the system gets. This data could be:

- Behavioural Data: What pages customers visit, what products they add to carts, or how long they spend on your site.

- Transactional Data: Purchase history, order frequency, and other buying habits.

- Customer Data: Age, location, preferences, and feedback.

2. Data Processing

Once the data's collected, it's cleaned up and organised. Think of it like sorting through a pile of receipts. The system prepares the data, makes sure it's usable, and organises it for the next step: decision-making.

3. Decision-Making

Now that the data's sorted, the agentic system can start making decisions:

- Predicting: For example, predicting what products a customer is likely to buy based on their browsing history and past purchases.

- Acting: Once the prediction is made, the system can take action, sending an offer, adjusting inventory, or re-engaging a lead.

- Adapting: If something changes (like a sudden sales spike or unexpected customer feedback), the system can adapt its actions in real time.

4. Continuous Improvement

What makes agentic systems so powerful is their ability to evolve. As the system receives more data, it learns, adapts, and refines its decision-making. Over time, it gets better at predicting, recommending, and making decisions based on the insights it gathers.

How to Build Our First Agentic System

Building our first agentic system doesn't have to be complicated.

Here's how we can get started:

1. Identify a Process to Automate

We need to look at our business processes. Which ones involve decision-making or could benefit from real-time data processing? For example, automating customer support, predicting demand for products, or lead scoring.

2. Choose the Right Platform

Pick a platform that's easy to use but powerful enough to handle our data and decisions. We need to look for:

- Built-in machine learning tools or APIs to train our system

- Simple integrations with our current CRM, eCommerce, or workflow tools

3. Feed Data Into the System

For the system to learn, we need to give it data. Whether it's behavioural data from our CRM or transactional data from our store, the system needs a constant stream of fresh information.

4. Define Decision Rules

Before our system can start learning, set some initial decision rules. These can be based on simple "if/then" statements. For example:

- If a customer opens an email, send a follow-up reminder after 48 hours.

- If a support ticket is not resolved in 24 hours, escalate it automatically.

5. Monitor & Refine

After launching our agentic system, we need to monitor how well it's performing. Check its decision accuracy, track outcomes, and gather feedback. The more data it processes, the better it becomes.

How to Build Our First Agentic System

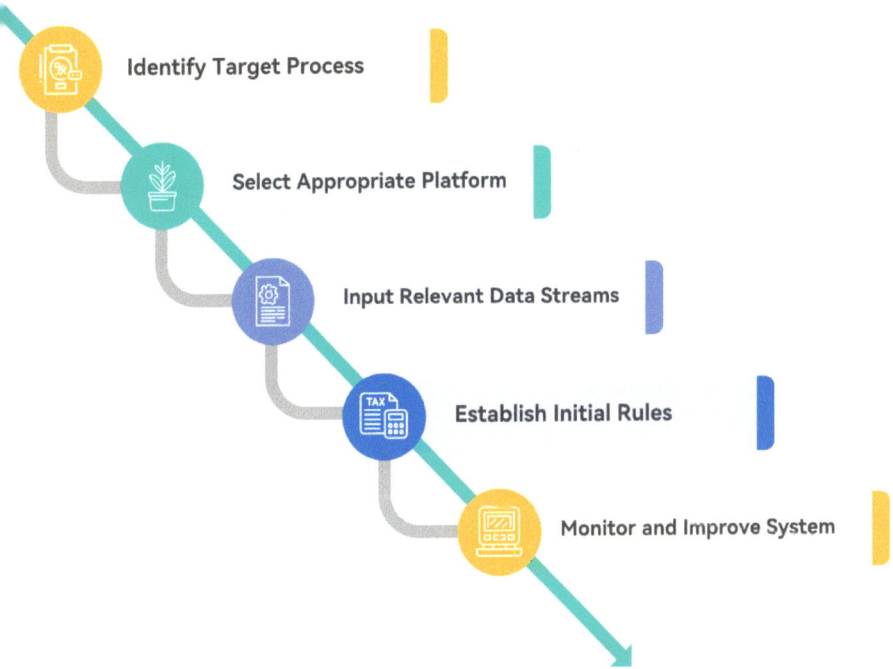

- Identify Target Process
- Select Appropriate Platform
- Input Relevant Data Streams
- Establish Initial Rules
- Monitor and Improve System

Best Practices for Implementing Agentic Systems Successfully

Now that we understand how agentic systems work and how they can transform our business, it's time to talk about ways that ensure our implementation is a success.

These are strategies that will not only help us get the most out of our agentic systems but also make sure they deliver lasting value.

Start with Clear Objectives and KPIs

Before we implement an agentic system, it's critical to define what success looks like. This might seem obvious, but too often businesses launch AI systems without specific goals or metrics to track.

- **Set clear, measurable KPIs** for the system. These could be things like response time, customer satisfaction, lead conversion rates, or operational efficiency improvements.

- **Monitor early performance:** Don't just wait for the system to run for months before evaluating it. Regularly check in on how well the system is hitting those targets.

Consider this:

If we're implementing an AI-driven chatbot for customer support, some KPIs to track could include:

- **Customer satisfaction scores (CSAT)**

- **Average response time** vs human agents

- **Escalation rate** (how often the bot needs human intervention)

Educate and Upskill the Team

Even the most sophisticated agentic system is only as good as the people using it. We need to make sure our team has the knowledge and training they need to work alongside the system and get the best results.

- **Create training resources:** Provide teams with hands-on guides for interacting with and monitoring the system, so they understand how to adjust, manage, and get the most out of it.

- **Host regular upskilling sessions:** Whether it's webinars, workshops, or small team meetings, give employees the space to ask questions, test features, and explore new possibilities.

Consider this:

If your sales team is using an agentic system for lead scoring, train them on how to adjust the criteria, review the lead prioritisation, and follow up with the highest-potential leads first. Ensure they're not just using the system, but optimising it.

Start Small and Scale Gradually

Implementing agentic systems at scale can be overwhelming, especially if we try to automate too many processes at once.

The key is to start with one process that's high impact but easy to measure, then expand as we get results.

- **Don't overcomplicate things early on:** Focus on one key area where the system will have the most immediate and measurable impact. Whether that's automating customer support, handling lead scoring, or managing inventory, keep it simple at first.

- **Refine and expand:** Once the first system has been refined and results begin to show, we can slowly scale and integrate more complex systems across other areas of our business.

Consider this:

When scaling our company globally, i4T Global realised that it needs to keep a close watch on competitor positioning.

We set up a competitor analysis agent that would visit our competitor sites every day, and when there is a change on their website, like a news announcement, a price update, or a feature release, it would automatically send us an email with a before-and-after visual site comparison.

Once this proved its efficacy, we later added an AI summary of the change along with an AI analysis of possible intent behind the change, helping us timely adjust our own strategy.

Avoid the "Set It and Forget It" Mentality

One of the biggest mistakes companies make with agentic systems is assuming that once they're up and running, they don't need to touch them again. In reality, agentic systems need ongoing monitoring and refinement.

- **Review performance regularly:** Monitor the system's performance metrics frequently to spot any issues or opportunities for improvement.

- **Adjust and retrain:** As our business grows or changes, so should our agentic systems. Make sure to update the data it uses, retrain the system as needed, and keep adapting to new customer behaviours, market trends, or seasonal shifts.

Consider this:

If our customer support chatbot is struggling to resolve certain types of issues, or if it starts answering incorrectly due to changes in your product, we'll need to retrain it with fresh data or revise the decision rules.
It's not a one-time job.

Prioritise Security and Data Privacy

Agentic systems rely heavily on customer data to make decisions, which means protecting that data is crucial. If we're handling sensitive customer information, we must ensure our system is compliant with data protection laws like GDPR or CCPA (California Consumer Privacy Act).

- **Data encryption:** Ensure that all customer data processed by the system is encrypted and stored securely.

- **Transparent data practices:** Make sure customers know how their data is being used and give them the option to opt out of certain types of data collection, if necessary.

- **Regular audits:** Run regular audits of the agentic systems to ensure they aren't inadvertently collecting unnecessary or excessive data.

Consider this:

For a work order management system used by strata managers, it is vital that all customer information that comes with a service request for maintenance is kept private and only used to enhance the user experience. At i4T Global, we ensure strict adherence to GDPR, ISO 27001, and other industry regulations, making data protection a core component of every solution. This commitment to security and transparency not only meets legal requirements but also helps build long-term customer trust.

Foster a Culture of Continuous Learning & Improvement

AI systems are not static; they evolve over time. But this requires an ongoing commitment to continuous learning and improvement. We need to encourage our teams to keep exploring new ways the system can be used and integrated.

- **Foster innovation:** Encourage employees to experiment with how AI can improve other processes in the business. Whether it's enhancing customer touchpoints or making internal processes more efficient, keep the conversation going about how AI can add value.

- **Create feedback loops:** Regularly gather feedback from users (customers, employees) to identify areas where the system can be improved.

Consider this:

Perhaps our agentic system is running customer support, and we realise that it could be used to anticipate common support queries before they even happen. Encouraging innovation like this leads to continuous value.

Measure Success and Refine Goals

Finally, always keep an eye on the results. Implement clear KPIs and track the system's performance against them. Regularly evaluate the impact it's having on the business.

- **Adjust KPIs over time:** As the system improves, our KPIs might need to evolve too.

- **Use data to refine the approach:** If we see any trends or patterns in how the system is working, we need to use that insight to optimise its decisions, adjust its rules, or add new data inputs.

Consider this:

If our AI-based sales assistant is successfully recommending products, but leads to higher cart abandonment rates, we may want to tweak the recommendations or include more information about the product in our suggestions.

Best Practices for Agentic AI Success

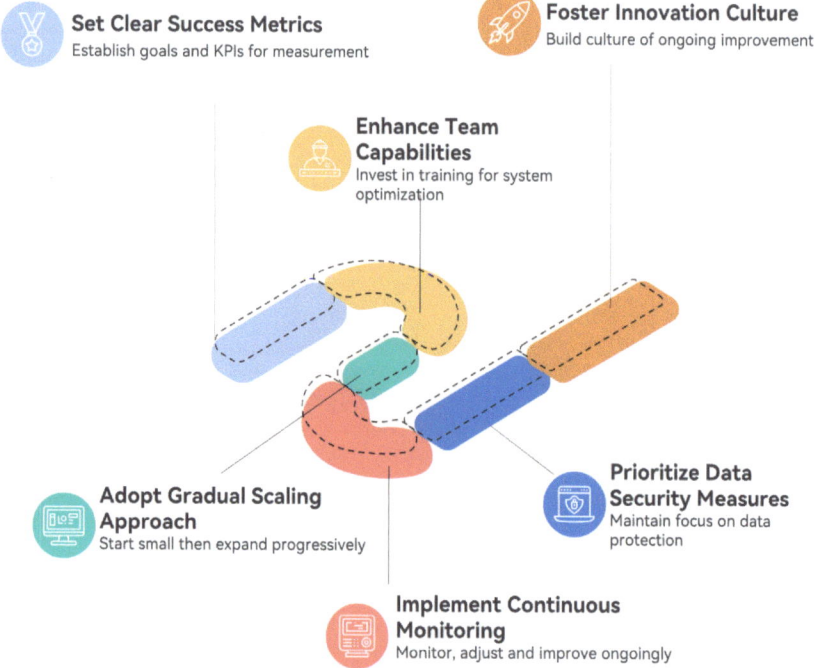

Best Practices for Agentic AI Success

Set Clear Success Metrics
Establish goals and KPIs for measurement

Foster Innovation Culture
Build culture of ongoing improvement

Enhance Team Capabilities
Invest in training for system optimization

Adopt Gradual Scaling Approach
Start small then expand progressively

Prioritize Data Security Measures
Maintain focus on data protection

Implement Continuous Monitoring
Monitor, adjust and improve ongoingly

By following these best practices, we can set our business up for long-term success with agentic systems, giving us the ability to scale efficiently, improve decision-making, and deliver smarter experiences.

Where Do We Go from Here?

The future of agentic systems isn't just about automating isolated tasks, it's about full business operations running autonomously, from the first customer interaction to final delivery.

End-to-End Business Operations

Imagine a world where our business can operate without human intervention in routine processes.

From marketing and sales to customer service and product delivery, autonomous systems will handle it all, making real-time decisions, adapting to customer needs, and adjusting workflows without the need for manual oversight.

Integration with AI-Driven Personalisation

The next frontier will see agentic systems working seamlessly with hyper-personalisation tools.

AI will not only decide when and how to engage with customers but also tailor every interaction based on customer history, preferences, and behaviour, creating deeply personal experiences at scale.

Continuous Improvement

What makes agentic systems truly powerful is their capacity to evolve.

These systems don't just perform tasks; they improve with every interaction. They learn from each customer touchpoint, adjust their actions, and continuously refine their decision-making, all without human input.

"The future isn't just about doing more with less. It's about doing more intelligently, with systems that think, learn, and act in ways that were once only human."

Chapter 06:

Continuous Learning as a Digital Culture in the Age of AI

In 2025, the question isn't whether we can learn, but how fast we can.

Back in 2015, when I wrote *Think Digital – The Ultimate Digital Transformation Guide for SMEs*, the call was clear: businesses needed to embrace technology to stay competitive. A decade later, the pace of change has only accelerated. With AI now reshaping every industry, disruption is no longer an occasional challenge - it's the permanent state of play.

Today, with a new AI tool hitting the market every few weeks, the most valuable skill any business can cultivate is the ability to keep learning.

Continuous learning is no longer optional; it's survival. Those who fail to adopt a learning mindset risk being outpaced by competitors, blindsided by market shifts, and locked out of the next wave of innovation.

Consider this:

- 94% of employees say they would stay longer at a company if it invested in their career development (LinkedIn, 2023).

- 70% of the skills employees need today will change in the next five years (World Economic Forum, 2024).

- Companies that nurture a learning culture are 92% more likely to innovate successfully, with employees 46% more likely to stay engaged and productive (McKinsey, 2023).

Continuous learning isn't just about keeping up with the latest trends. It's about building a culture that can adapt, pivot, and evolve as quickly as the challenges and opportunities around you change.

A business that fosters a learning culture isn't static; it's dynamic, resilient, and innovative.

In this chapter, we'll explore how we can create a learning organisation, where learning isn't just a department function or an afterthought. It's a core part of our business strategy.

In the age of AI, the only way to stay ahead is to learn faster than the competition.

The Need for a Learning Culture in a Digital World

Why staying static in a fast-moving world isn't an option anymore in the age of AI.

In today's world, businesses are faced with constant digital disruption. Technology is evolving at a rate that's almost impossible to keep up with, and the skills required to operate and thrive in this new landscape are changing faster than ever.

To stay ahead, businesses need to embrace continuous learning as a core component of their culture. Not just in terms of new AI tools we adopt, but also learning lessons from our successes and failures.

An Era Where Change Is The Only Constant

The pace of AI innovation and adoption is accelerating at an unprecedented rate.

Research from the World Economic Forum reveals that 70% of the skills employees need today will change in the next five years. That's a significant shift, and it signals just how quickly companies need to adapt to stay relevant.

Businesses that were once comfortable with traditional, one-off training programs are now realising that learning isn't a one-time event; it's an ongoing process.

Why is this important?

In this AI era, skills can quickly become outdated. New technologies, systems, and platforms are introduced at lightning speed, making traditional job roles, tools, and workflows obsolete. The companies that will thrive are those that continuously reskill and upskill their teams with upcoming AI trends and stay ahead of the curve by learning as they go.

The Risks of Stagnation

As industries continue to evolve, companies that fail to keep pace with technological advancements risk:

- **Lagging in innovation:** Without continuous learning, businesses can't adapt to emerging trends or customer demands.

- **Skill gaps:** Employees who haven't kept up with new AI technologies can't execute at their full potential.

- **Employee disengagement:** Teams want to work for organisations that invest in their growth. Without learning opportunities, talent retention becomes difficult.

The reality is, businesses that don't prioritise learning aren't just falling behind, they're becoming obsolete.

If we're not learning, we're not growing, and if we're not growing, someone else, implementing AI better and faster than us, is taking our place.

Learning Drives Innovation and Adaptability

One of the key reasons continuous learning is essential is that it fosters innovation. When employees are constantly learning and adapting to new AI tools, processes, and ideas, they are more likely to think creatively and push boundaries.

Companies that prioritise AI learning:

- **Foster a growth mindset:** Employees feel empowered to take risks, try new things, and solve problems in innovative ways, thanks to low-code/no-code solutions.

- Improve adaptability: The business can respond quickly to changes in the market, customer needs, or technological advancements, with AI-powered decision-making.

- Leverage knowledge effectively: When everyone is encouraged to learn and share insights, the company's collective knowledge base grows exponentially.

Companies that build a culture of learning inspire employees to think beyond their day-to-day tasks and look for opportunities to innovate. This mindset isn't just about keeping up with competitors; it's about leading the pack by thinking ahead of the curve.

The Role of Leadership in Fostering a Learning Culture

Leaders play a crucial role in creating and nurturing a learning culture. When executives and managers encourage continuous learning, invest in employee development, and model learning behaviours themselves, they signal to the rest of the organisation that learning is a priority.

What does this look like in practice?

- **Investing in development programs:** Offering AI training, access to AI courses, or dedicated time for learning new AI skills.

- **Promoting knowledge sharing:** Creating opportunities for employees to share insights, lessons, and AI best practices across teams.

- **Leading by example:** Leaders who embrace learning themselves, by attending courses, reading industry books, or engaging in peer learning, set the AI tone for the rest of the organisation.

Companies that invest in employee learning are 92% more likely to succeed in their innovation efforts. (McKinsey)

7 Steps to Building the Foundations of a Continuous Learning Culture

Creating a continuous learning culture towards AI requires commitment and consistency, but it doesn't have to be complex.

Here's how we, at i4T Global laid the foundation for a thriving learning culture in our AI-powered business:

Step 1. Define Learning as a Core Value

We started by making learning a priority at every level of the business. We communicated the importance of continuous learning, and ensured leadership led by example. We integrate "continuous learning" into our mission and values, making it clear that adopting AI was not just a department function but a business-wide commitment.

Step 2. Create Structured Learning Opportunities

We implemented an AI learning calendar that included regular workshops, training, and knowledge-sharing sessions. This meant offering varied formats (e.g., on-demand courses, peer-to-peer learning, webinars) so every employee had access to resources that suited their learning style.

Step 3. Foster Self-Directed Learning

We encourage employees to take ownership of their learning. We started this by offering self-learning hours and a curated list of resources on AI (books, articles, courses), which helped our team build their AI skills on their own. This ensured we supported personal learning goals for each employee.

Step 4. Implement Knowledge Sharing

We established systems for employees to share their AI knowledge across teams. We did this through peer mentorship programs and internal knowledge hubs to encourage collaboration and learning from each other's experiences.

Step 5. Use Technology to Scale Learning

We leveraged technology like LMS platforms and AI-driven learning tools to provide personalised learning paths and resources. This ensured that learning could scale with our team as it grows.

Step 6. Measure and Track Learning Success

We have defined KPIs for learning (e.g., completion rates, AI skill improvements, engagement) and track these regularly. We gather feedback from employees to ensure that the learning initiatives are effective and make adjustments as needed.

Step 7. Overcome Barriers and Encourage Adoption

Lastly, we addressed any barriers to learning, such as a lack of time or resources. Celebrating learning achievements and creating a recognition program keep our team engaged and motivated.

For a more detailed, actionable approach, refer to the Learning Culture Self-Assessment in the appendix. This series of questions will help you identify the gaps and guide your team through the process of building a continuous learning culture, and help you track your progress.

7 Steps to Building the Foundations of a Continuous Learning Culture

Overcome Adoption Barriers
The seventh step works to overcome barriers and encourage adoption of learning practices

Use Tech for Scaling
The fifth step utilizes technology to scale up the reach of learning initiatives

Measure Learning Success
The sixth step involves measuring and tracking the success of learning efforts

Foster Self-Directed
The third step focuses on fostering self-directed and independent learning behaviors

Implement Knowledge Share
The fourth step is to implement systems for sharing knowledge among members

Define Core Value
The first step is to define learning as a fundamental core value for the organization

Create Structured Ops
The second step involves creating structured opportunities for learning activities

Leveraging Technology to Drive Continuous Learning

Learning doesn't happen in a vacuum.

To create a truly continuous AI learning culture, we need the right tools to scale and personalise learning experiences, making them accessible and engaging for every employee.

Luckily, we live in a time where technology is perfectly positioned to accelerate and amplify learning. From AI-driven platforms to Learning Management Systems (LMS), technology helps businesses integrate learning into daily workflows, ensuring it happens seamlessly.

Use a Learning Management System (LMS) to Centralise Learning

A Learning Management System (LMS) is a central hub where all our learning content, courses, and materials live. It makes learning more accessible, organised, and trackable.

An LMS helps organise training content, track employee progress, and offer flexible learning options at scale. With the right LMS, employees can access courses, assessments, and certifications at their own pace, anywhere, anytime.

Here's what we learned along the way:

- It helps when we choose an LMS that fits our company's needs and integrates with our existing tools.

- Upload core training materials and track learning progress. We can even gamify learning experiences to keep employees engaged and motivated.

Leverage AI to Personalise Learning

When all our processes are benefiting from AI, why should employee learning be left behind?

AI can personalise learning experiences based on individual needs. By analysing an employee's progress, interests, and skills, AI can suggest learning paths and resources tailored specifically for them.

This makes learning more relevant and impactful, rather than a one-size-fits-all approach.

Here's what we learned along the way:

- Look for AI-driven learning platforms that use algorithms to suggest personalised learning content for employees.

- Regularly update the AI with new data to ensure the system stays accurate and effective.

Integrate Microlearning for Quick, Bite-Sized Training

In the world of digital learning, microlearning is a big win. Microlearning breaks down content into small, focused units that employees can quickly consume, without overwhelming them. This method is ideal for embedding learning into the flow of daily work.

Employees can learn in small doses, ideal for fitting into busy schedules. Whether it's a 5-minute video or a short quiz, microlearning can reinforce key concepts and skills without taking too much time.

Here's what we learned along the way:

- Create bite-sized content (like short tutorials, videos, or quizzes) and deliver it regularly.

- Distribute microlearning materials across channels employees already use (email, chat, your LMS, etc.).

Use Collaborative Tools for Social Learning

Learning doesn't have to be a solo activity. Collaborative learning enables employees to learn from each other, share knowledge, and work together to solve problems. Tools like Slack, Microsoft Teams, or internal forums can be great platforms for knowledge sharing.

When employees collaborate and share insights, it encourages peer-to-peer learning and creates a community of learners within your company. Social learning also makes the learning experience more interactive and less formal.

Here's what we learned along the way:

- We can start by encouraging employees to share resources, insights, and experiences through shared platforms.

- This also creates spaces where employees can ask questions, brainstorm ideas, and collaborate on solving business challenges.

Track Progress and Improve with Learning Analytics

To continuously improve our learning culture, we need to measure how well our learning initiatives are working. Learning analytics lets us track employee progress, engagement, and overall effectiveness of our learning programs.

Learning analytics provide real-time insights into what's working and what's not, so we can make data-driven decisions. This ensures our learning efforts are aligned with company goals and employee needs.

Here's what we learned along the way:

- We can use our LMS or AI tools to gather data on employee participation, course completion rates, and performance.

- Regularly review this data to refine learning paths, content, and goals. Make adjustments based on feedback and performance trends.

Encourage Mobile Learning for Flexibility

Learning shouldn't be confined to the office or a desktop. Mobile learning offers the flexibility for employees to access learning content on the go, whether they're commuting, traveling, or working remotely.

Mobile learning increases accessibility and convenience, allowing employees to learn when it fits into their schedule. It also increases engagement by removing barriers to learning.

Here's what we learned along the way:

- Choose learning platforms that are mobile-friendly or have dedicated apps for easy access.
- Encourage employees to use their mobile devices for quick learning sessions, like watching videos or taking quizzes during downtime.

The key to leveraging technology for continuous learning is finding the right tools that meet our team's specific needs. Too many platforms can overwhelm employees. We can choose tools that integrate well with our existing systems and help employees learn in the way that suits them best.

Encouraging Cross-Departmental Learning and Collaboration

The power of learning doesn't just live within one department. When our teams come together, share knowledge, and solve problems collaboratively, the entire business benefits.

Encouraging cross-departmental learning not only boosts employee skills but also creates a dynamic, innovative workforce that thrives in today's fast-moving business world.

Smash Those Silos

Silos are the enemy of collaboration and growth. When departments don't communicate or learn from each other, the company misses out on valuable insights and opportunities for improvement. It's time to open the doors and bring teams together.

To tackle this, we can set up cross-departmental brainstorming sessions or workshops where employees from different areas work together to solve a challenge or share knowledge. This fosters a deeper understanding of how the whole business operates, not just individual departments.

Make Mentorship Cross-Functional

Mentorship shouldn't be limited to one department. Pair employees from different areas to collaborate on projects and share their expertise. When someone from marketing shares insights with someone from sales, or a support rep teaches product specialists a new approach, magic happens. The whole team becomes smarter, together.

Cross-functional mentorship programs are where employees from diverse departments team up to exchange skills, experiences, and best practices.

Use Tools that Make Sharing Easy

Great collaboration requires great tools. Platforms like Slack, Teams, or Notion are perfect for breaking down silos. Set up channels or groups dedicated to specific topics, so employees from different teams can easily share insights, resources, or solutions to challenges. Knowledge-sharing shouldn't feel like a chore; it should be easy, natural, and fun.

We can create a knowledge-sharing hub on our preferred platform, where employees can drop in resources, ask questions, or highlight success stories from their departments.

Build a Culture of Feedback and Reflection

Learning thrives on feedback and reflection. When employees regularly exchange feedback across teams, they learn from one another's experiences, build stronger working relationships, and improve processes faster. Make feedback a regular part of work culture, not just something that happens in annual reviews.

Incorporate reflection sessions into team meetings, where departments share what's worked, what hasn't, and what they've learned from cross-team collaboration. This makes learning a living, breathing part of our culture.

Measuring and Tracking Continuous Learning

We've created the learning structures, encouraged our teams to get involved, and started building a culture of continuous improvement. But how do we know it's working?

How can we track progress and measure success in a way that drives real change? Measuring and tracking learning outcomes doesn't have to be complicated. The key is to make sure our approach is clear, measurable, and aligned with our business goals.

This allows us to stay on top of our efforts and continuously refine our strategy.

Measuring and Tracking Continuous Learning

Step	What to Track	Actions
Set Clear, Actionable KPIs	• Employee participation • Skill development • Business impact	Define KPIs and track them regularly.
Track Learning Progress and Completion Rates	• Completion rates • Job performance • Time to proficiency	Review these after training.
Gather Feedback From Employees	• Satisfaction with learning materials • Feedback on learning formats • Barriers to participation	Collect feedback to refine learning programs.

Measure Knowledge Retention and Application	• Knowledge retention • Performance metrics before and after training • Self-reported application of learning	Conduct regular assessments.
Review the Business Impact of Learning Initiatives	• Employee Efficiency • Business Revenue • Customer satisfaction • Innovation outcomes	Assess the impact of learning on business KPIs
Create Regular Feedback Loops	• Learning completion rates, performance improvements, feedback from managers	Set up quarterly reviews and adjust training programs.

Overcoming Barriers to a Learning Culture

Building a continuous learning culture is powerful, but it's not always easy. And we witnessed this first-hand at i4T Global.

The journey is somewhat for most businesses.

We encounter obstacles that can slow down or even derail our efforts to embed learning across the organisation.

Lack of Time and Resources

One of the biggest barriers to learning we experienced was time; employees were already stretched thin with their day-to-day tasks, and adding "learning" to their already-packed schedules seemed like an impossible task.

Here's what worked for us

We integrated learning into daily workflows by offering bite-sized content (e.g., microlearning) and flexible learning hours, making it easy to learn without disrupting work.

Resistance to Change

Employees who are used to a certain way of working may feel resistant to the idea of constant learning or adopting new tools. Change fatigue is a real challenge, especially in environments where change happens quickly.

This resistance is not just limited to internal teams but can also be a barrier to the customer base, especially for technology service providers like i4T Global. While larger corporate software companies have already tackled this challenge, there may soon be a need to address it more aggressively to stay competitive.

Here's what worked for us

We communicated the benefits of learning clearly, showing how it aligns with both personal growth and business success, and started small to build momentum.

Limited Access to Learning Resources

In some businesses, the learning resources available may be outdated, irrelevant, or simply hard to access. Without the right tools and content, it's tough to foster a robust learning culture.

Here's what worked for us

We curated and centralised relevant learning materials, making sure they are easily accessible and up to date, and created a knowledge hub that employees can easily tap into.

Fear of Failing or Making Mistakes

In any learning process, there's a risk of failure, but the fear of failure can hold employees back from engaging with learning initiatives. They may worry about wasting time, making mistakes, or looking unprepared in front of their peers.

Here's what worked for us

We focused on fostering a growth mindset by celebrating mistakes as opportunities to learn and improve, ensuring employees feel safe to experiment.

Lack of Leadership Buy-In

If senior leadership doesn't buy into the idea of continuous learning, it can be tough to get the rest of the company on board. Without leadership support, employees may feel that learning initiatives aren't a priority.

Here's what worked for us

I, as the founder, got involved from the start, aligning learning with business goals and ensuring I lead by example to encourage wider buy-in across the organisation.

Limited Tracking and Recognition of Learning Efforts

In many businesses, learning efforts go untracked and unrecognised, which can lead to disengagement. Without clear rewards or recognition, employees may feel that their efforts are going unnoticed.

Here's what worked for us

We closely tracked learning outcomes, and I made it a point to publicly recognise achievements, incorporating learning milestones into performance reviews and reward systems.

Overwhelming Amount of Content

Sometimes, employees feel overwhelmed by the sheer volume of content available. When there are too many courses, workshops, or resources to choose from, it can be difficult to know where to start, leading to decision fatigue.

Here's what worked for us

We are trying to address this barrier by curating focused learning paths based on role-specific goals, ensuring employees can easily find the most relevant content for their growth.

The Future of Continuous Learning in Business

The future of business lies in its ability to adapt quickly, and continuous learning is the key to this agility.

Moreover, businesses now require initiatives to come from the ground up, more than ever before, rather than waiting for management to drive change. Relying solely on top-down mandates can often be too slow, leaving customers struggling to remain competitive.

For software providers like i4T Global, we have seen it firsthand how critical it can be to act in line with the timing of these evolving needs, ensuring we are the right partner to help our clients adapt swiftly and effectively.

By embracing technology, fostering a culture of curiosity, and ensuring learning is deeply embedded in everyday work, companies can stay ahead of disruptions, fuel innovation, and empower their teams.

As learning evolves, businesses that prioritise it will be able to not only keep up with change but also lead it.

Chapter 07:

Digital Maturity Self-Assessment

Let's imagine for a moment we're planning a road trip across Australia. We've got our playlist sorted, snacks packed, and our destination all punched in. But there's just one small problem. We never figured out where we're starting from.

Sounds like a disaster waiting to happen, right? And yet, that's exactly what many businesses do when it comes to digital transformation. We dive into new tools, rush into AI, or launch a shiny app, without ever stopping to ask: Where are we right now?

AI isn't something we just install. It demands a certain level of digital maturity to be effective and not disruptive in the wrong ways.

For i4T Global, the AI adoption journey wasn't too different. We knew we had already arrived at the peak of our digital maturity. But where do we go from there, except for further expanding our platform's capabilities?

And just then, AI came knocking. We knew AI was where we wanted to head next. But there were a series of questions that needed to be asked first.

- Where do we stand right now?
- What do we want to be in the next couple of years?
- Do we have what it takes to be there?
- How do we get there?

That's what this chapter is all about. It's your digital map check. Your moment of clarity before the acceleration begins.

Because here's the truth: transformation isn't just about moving fast. It's about moving smart, and that means knowing your current capabilities, your gaps, and your hidden strengths.

The goal isn't to score top marks. The goal is honest reflection. To take a breath, zoom out, and understand the digital DNA of your business today, so we can shape the right strategy for tomorrow.

Whether you're running a solo consultancy, leading a mid-sized retail operation, or building a startup with global dreams, this self-assessment will give you a crystal-clear snapshot of where you stand across five key areas: strategy, people, process, technology, and culture.

Let's find out where our business sits on the digital maturity curve, and what that means for our next big move.

The 5 Pillars of Digital Maturity

Digital transformation isn't just about the tech we buy; it's about the business we build.

Before we dive headfirst into AI, automation, or the next big platform, let's hit pause and ask: how ready is our business, really? Because true transformation only sticks when the five core areas: **our strategy, our people, our processes, our tech, and our culture**, are working together like a well-oiled machine.

Let's break it down.

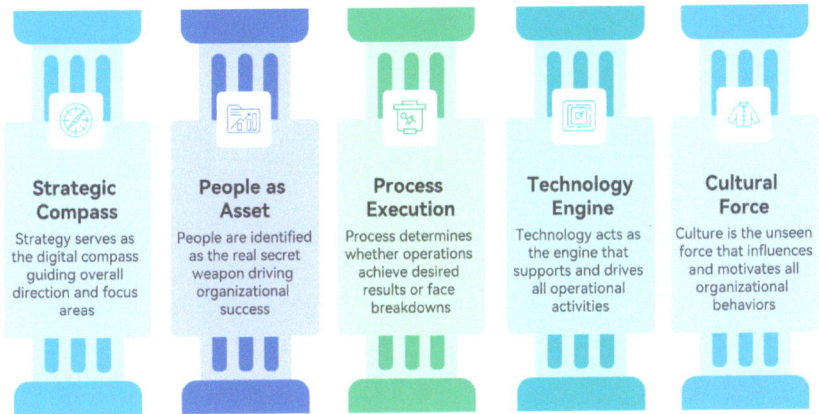

Strategic Compass	People as Asset	Process Execution	Technology Engine	Cultural Force
Strategy serves as the digital compass guiding overall direction and focus areas	People are identified as the real secret weapon driving organizational success	Process determines whether operations achieve desired results or face breakdowns	Technology acts as the engine that supports and drives all operational activities	Culture is the unseen force that influences and motivates all organizational behaviors

Pillar 1: Strategy – Our Digital Compass

"If digital's not in the plan, it's not in the business."

We need to think of strategy like our business GPS. Without it, we're just spinning wheels and burning cash.

A solid digital strategy is more than a buzzword brainstorm or a once-a-year boardroom slide deck. It's a living, breathing roadmap that links our tech moves to our business goals, and makes sure everyone's paddling in the same direction.

What great looks like:

- We've got a clear digital vision, not just a wishlist.

- Our strategy talks about results, like "increase conversions" or "slash admin time".

- We review and refresh regularly.

- Everyone, from the intern to the MD, knows what winning looks like digitally.

Questions We Need to Ask:

- Are we solving real problems?

- Do we have a game plan, or are we playing catch-up with competitors?

Pillar 2: People – Our Real Secret Weapon

"Tech doesn't transform businesses; people do."

AI can't build trust, win customers, or lead a team. Only people can.

This pillar is all about digital confidence, skills, and leadership. Our team doesn't need to be full of coders or data scientists, but they do need to be curious, capable, and ready to roll with change.

What great looks like:

- As a leader, we walk the digital talk. We don't just delegate it.

- We build a learning culture where upskilling is part of the job.

- Teams collaborate across roles and departments using smart tools.

- People are empowered to innovate, rather than being bogged down in bureaucracy.

Questions We Need to Ask:

- Are we training for the future or surviving the now?

- Is digital seen as "everyone's job" or just IT's headache?

Pillar 3: Process – Where the Magic Happens (or Falls Apart)

"Great tools won't fix broken processes."

We've all seen it. Someone installs a fancy new system... and it ends up collecting dust while staff go back to spreadsheets and sticky notes.

This pillar is all about how smoothly our business runs behind the scenes, and whether our workflows help or hinder our goals.

What great looks like:

- Repetitive tasks? Automated. Bottlenecks? Eliminated.

- Our systems talk to each other. No more double-handling or email tag.

- We can adapt quickly when things shift, whether it's a new regulation or a customer demand.

- Our processes scale with the business, not slow it down.

Questions We Need to Ask:

- Are we using digital tools to do the same old thing faster, or doing better things altogether?

- Is our customer journey smooth... or stitched together with duct tape?

Pillar 4: Technology – The Engine Under the Hood

"More tools? No thanks. Smarter tools? Yes, please."

This is where most businesses start, but it's rarely where the real problems lie. Tech is the enabler, not the hero. The real question isn't "what tools do we have?" It's "What are they helping us do?"

What great looks like:
- Our platforms are integrated, not isolated. One login, one source of truth.

- We've got strong data foundations; clean, real-time, and reliable.

- AI, automation, and cloud tools are part of our workflow.

- Cybersecurity is active, up-to-date, and taken seriously by everyone.

Questions We Need to Ask:
- Are we choosing tech that fits our strategy?

- Is our tech stack helping us move faster?

Pillar 5: Culture – The Invisible Force That Drives Everything

"We don't rise to the level of our tech. We fall to the level of our culture."
Culture is what people do when no one's watching. It's our company's attitude toward change, learning, risk-taking, and yes, even failure.

If our team's scared to test, try, or speak up, we'll never get real digital traction. On the flip side, a curious, open, adaptable culture? That's rocket fuel.

What great looks like:
- People ask "what if?" instead of "what now?"

- Learning is baked with micro-trainings, shared insights, and open debriefs.

- Wins are celebrated. So are lessons from things that didn't quite land.

- Change is embraced, not endured.

Questions We Need to Ask:
- Are we leading with curiosity, or clinging to "how we've always done it"?

- Does innovation happen here... or walk out the door?

Together, these five pillars give us a full-body scan of our business's digital health, not just its appearance, but its muscle, movement, and mindset.

The Self-Assessment Framework

We've just explored the five critical pillars of digital maturity. Now comes the moment of truth: where does our business really stand?

This framework isn't a corporate quiz or a shiny leaderboard. It's a clarity tool. And in a world moving faster than ever, clarity is everything.

This self-assessment tool, which we built for our own internal use at i4T Global, is designed for teams who want to work smarter, not harder, and who are ready to face the facts so they can actually start transforming.

Here's where we'll assess our business across the five pillars we just dissected:

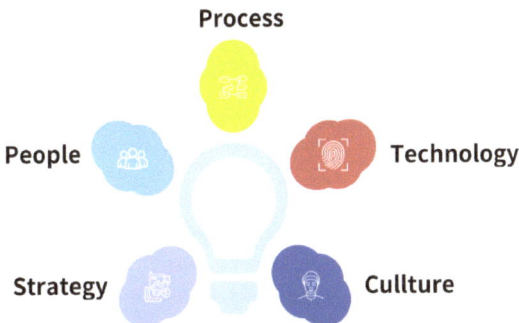

For each one, we rated ourselves honestly on a scale from 1 to 5 and used the scoring guide below to calibrate.

Scores vary across team members. That's insight in itself. The important thing is to use this tool to start conversations, not just collect numbers.

The Scoring Scale

Score	What It Means
1 – Early Days	We're just beginning this journey. There's little clarity, no formal strategy, and digital is more idea than action. Mostly reactive.
2 – Patchy Progress	Some efforts are happening, but they're inconsistent, siloed, or leader-dependent. We've got a few wins, but no real rhythm.
3 – On the Move	We've got traction. There's a sense of direction, some systems in place, and signs of alignment, but lots of room to sharpen and scale.
4 – Solid Foundations	We're confident. Digital is integrated across most of the business. Tools and processes are humming, the team's engaged, and results are showing.
5 – Leading the Charge	Digital is how we operate. We're nimble, data-led, customer-focused, and future-ready. We test, learn, and adapt like it's second nature.

Digital Maturity Scorecard

It's time to fill in the scores and jot down key notes or friction points. When scoring as a team, we must compare responses. Remember, alignment here is gold.

Pillar	Your Score (1–5)	Quick Notes / Observations
Strategy		Do we have a clear, living digital roadmap? Are our digital moves tied to business goals?
People		Do our people have the skills and mindset for digital? Are leaders walking the talk?
Process		Are we still relying on workarounds and manual fixes, or are things smooth, automated, and scalable?
Technology		Are our tools integrated, effective, and ready for the next wave (AI, automation, etc.)?
Culture		Are we curious and adaptable? Do we embrace change or fear it?
TOTAL	/25	

How to Use The Scores

This scorecard gave us both a big picture and laser focus.

Here's how we made the most of it, and you can too!

1. Don't Obsess Over the Total

If we scored 18/25, but our Process is a 2? That's our weak link. Addressing that gap will create ripple effects everywhere else.

2. Treat Each Pillar Like a Leverage Point

We realised we don't need to be a 5 in every category tomorrow. So we looked at where small improvements could unlock big outcomes. Often, strengthening just one area can elevate the rest.

3. Reflect as a Team

If we're not doing this solo, we must bring our leadership or core team together. So we asked where our scores differ. Why? These are the conversations that surface blind spots and hidden strengths.

Interpreting The Results

Remember, it's not about where we are on the map, it's knowing that we're on the map.

We've done the work. We've scored each pillar, reflected on how our business stacks up, and perhaps even had a few honest conversations with our team.

Now it's time to make sense of the numbers.

This isn't about putting the business into a box. It's about understanding the stage we're in so we can make the right decisions next, not based on hype or pressure, but on our business's real readiness.

Let's decode this score and unpack what each stage means, what's likely working, what might be holding us back, and where to focus next.

Score: 5–10 — Stage: Early Days

At this stage, we're at the beginning of our digital journey. We may have some digital tools in place, a basic website, a few social media posts, maybe even a cloud-based invoicing system, but there's no overarching strategy or alignment.

Digital efforts likely feel reactive or experimental, driven by urgency or external pressure (COVID, competitor moves, or customer demand). There may be hesitation internally; some team members might resist change, or you're simply unsure where to begin.

What's Working:
- We're aware that change is needed; that's step one.

- There are often one or two passionate individuals pushing for progress.

- We may already be online and collecting customer data (even if it's messy).

Common Challenges at This Stage:

- No clear digital roadmap or vision.

- Decisions are made in silos or based on gut feeling, not data.

- Tech tools are underused, disconnected, or outdated.

- Little to no automation; manual processes dominate.

Areas We Need to Focus on:

- Start simple. Identify 1–2 "quick win" projects, like automating client bookings or improving online visibility.

- Assign digital ownership to a dedicated internal champion.

- Upskill ourselves and the team in digital basics (e.g., cloud tools, data literacy, collaboration platforms).

- Begin documenting customer touchpoints and common pain points.

Tools Anyone Can Start with Right Now:

- Google Workspace or Microsoft 365 for cloud collaboration.

- Canva for basic brand design.

- Mailchimp or ActiveCampaign for email marketing automation.

Score: 11–15 — Stage: Patchy Progress

We're in the midst of a transition. The business is starting to embrace digital, but it's inconsistent. Some teams may be flying ahead with tools and ideas, while others are stuck in analogue land.

We've moved beyond awareness and into action, but the foundation still needs reinforcing.

There's usually some success to point to (a CRM rollout, social media wins, cloud tools adoption), but it hasn't yet translated into a holistic transformation.

What's Working:

- We've got systems in place, but they might not be integrated.

- Some processes are being automated, and results are improving.

- Team members are starting to show digital confidence.

- Leadership may be open to digital, even if not fully committed yet.

Common Challenges at This Stage:

- Lack of a single, unifying digital strategy.

- Teams working in silos.

- Decisions often still hinge on individuals rather than systems.

- Customer experience is still inconsistent across channels.

Areas We Need to Focus on:

- Develop a digital roadmap that spans all departments.

- Invest in integration so that data flows smoothly.

- Run cross-functional workshops to break silos and foster alignment.

- Begin using data to inform decision-making.

Tools To Level Up:

- Asana, Trello, or ClickUp for team visibility and project coordination.

- Zapier or Make for automating repetitive tasks.

- HubSpot CRM or Zoho for centralising customer data.

Score: 16–20 — Stage: On the Move

We've built solid foundations. Our team uses digital tools with confidence, automation is saving time, and our systems talk to each other (mostly).

We're tracking performance and maybe even starting to explore emerging tech like AI or low-code tools.

But... we're not done yet.

This is the sweet spot where we're poised to shift from operational improvement to strategic innovation.

What's Working:

- Strategy, people, and technology are generally aligned.

- We're measuring key digital metrics and using data to optimise.

- There's an appetite for experimentation and calculated risk-taking.

- Customers are engaging across digital channels and coming back.

Common Challenges at This Stage:

- Data may be trapped in silos or not fully actioned.

- The culture may support innovation in pockets, but not business-wide.

- AI and advanced tools are on the radar, but not yet deployed with intent.

- Talent development may not be keeping pace with technology adoption.

Areas We Need to Focus on:

- Double down on customer experience like personalisation, predictive service, seamless UX.

- Integrate more advanced analytics to drive smarter decisions.

- Empower team leaders to champion innovation in their departments.

- Begin formalising AI pilot projects with clear metrics for success.

Tools We'll Want to Explore at This Stage:

- Notion or Monday.com for dashboards, planning, and knowledge sharing.

- AI copilots in customer service (e.g., Intercom, Drift) or content creation (e.g., Jasper, ChatGPT).

- Business intelligence tools like Google Looker Studio or Power BI.

Score: 21–25 — Stage: Solid Foundations

This is digital leadership in motion. We're already using technology strategically. Our people are skilled and agile, our systems are integrated, and our culture supports learning, experimentation, and speed.

We're likely exploring next-gen tools like agentic systems, autonomous workflows, or predictive analytics. Now our focus shifts to sustainability, scalability, and impact.

What's Working:
- Digital transformation is a mindset, not just a milestone.

- Innovation comes from across the business, not just the top.

- We're data-rich, insight-driven, and agile in our execution.

- We're seen as a digital leader in our industry or niche.

Common Challenges At This Stage:
- Avoiding digital fatigue or over-engineering processes.

- Ensuring ethical, inclusive, and secure tech usage.

- Keeping your innovation flywheel spinning as we grow.

- Maintaining a strong culture as new tools and people join the mix.

Areas We Need to Focus On:
- Formalise our AI and automation strategy (if we haven't already).

- Partner with other digital-first businesses to share knowledge and scale.

- Launch internal innovation programs (hackathons, reverse mentoring, etc.).

- Focus on ESG-driven tech solutions that align with long-term impact goals.

Tools We'll Need to Adopt at this Stage:
- CDPs (Customer Data Platforms) for personalisation at scale.

- Agentic AI platforms for automating complex decisions.

- Custom low-code apps for unique business models and workflows.

Wherever you landed, remember: digital maturity is not about "keeping up"; it's about creating momentum that fits your business, our team, and your market.

We must revisit this scorecard every 6–12 months, make it a leadership ritual, and let it evolve as our business evolves.

And most importantly, keep moving.

AI is a moving target. Even when we saw all departments actively using AI in their everyday task and building new AI-driven solutions for our clients, like the launch of "Yara AI" for PropTech and FSM sections, we are still learning new things every day, to create an even solid foundation for an AI-led future.

Common Pitfalls in Self-Assessment

Self-assessment is powerful, but only if done with honesty, humility, and a clear head. And let's face it, even the savviest businesses can fall into a few common traps that throw their digital maturity score off course.

Let's shine a light on the big three.

1. Confusing Tech Adoption with Transformation

Just because we've got a shiny new CRM, a chatbot on our homepage, or a Canva subscription doesn't mean we've transformed. Buying tools is easy. Integrating them meaningfully into our business? That's the real game.

The reality: Transformation isn't about what we've bought; it's about what we've changed. Have our processes improved? Are we making better decisions, serving customers faster, or reducing costs?

Ask yourself: Are our digital tools solving problems, or just adding noise?

2. Overestimating Digital Fluency

Here's a classic: "Oh, our team's pretty digital. We use Slack!"

Nice start. But true digital fluency goes deeper. It's about how confidently our team navigates data, learns new tools, collaborates virtually, and adapts to change.

The reality: Many businesses assume their people are more digitally savvy than they really are. It's not about age. It's about mindset and support. If team members are quietly Googling "how to use Teams" every day, that's a sign.

Ask yourself: Do our people feel confident using tech, or are they just surviving it?

3. Underestimating the Importance of Culture and People

Even with perfect tools and processes, nothing changes if the culture resists it. If people fear failure, hate change, or don't feel heard, transformation stalls before it starts.

The reality: Culture is the multiplier. A curious, open team will figure out new tech. A fearful, rigid one won't. That's why this pillar can't be skipped or sugar-coated.

Ask yourself: Do we reward experimentation, or only perfection?

Digital transformation is not a checkbox or a shopping list; it's a mindset shift. The more honest we are in our self-assessment, the more useful this whole exercise becomes.

So if one has accidentally fallen into one of these traps, don't worry. Spotting it now means you're already doing better than most.

If there's one thing this chapter has hopefully made clear, it's this: digital maturity isn't about being flashy, it's about being ready.

Before we introduce AI, before we automate workflows, before we launch that next campaign, we've got to know where we are, where we're strong, and where we're stuck.

Digital Maturity: 5 Truths to Lead By

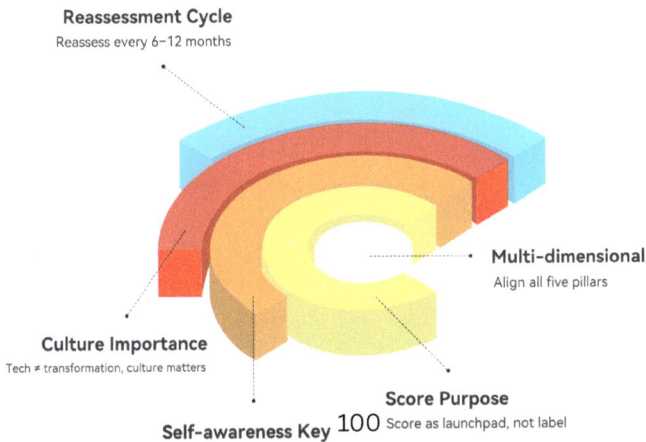

Reassessment Cycle
Reassess every 6–12 months

Multi-dimensional
Align all five pillars

Culture Importance
Tech ≠ transformation, culture matters

Score Purpose
Score as launchpad, not label

Self-awareness Key 100

Chapter 08:

Proven 90-Day AI Adoption Roadmap for SMEs

So far, I've discussed how digital transformation is vital for staying competitive. Whether it's automating processes, improving customer engagement, or creating a learning culture, every step I've taken in my business has been about building a stronger digital foundation.

But here's the next big step: **AI.**

For small and medium-sized enterprises (SMEs), artificial intelligence (AI) is no longer a tool that only the big players can afford. With affordable and user-friendly tools, AI has become accessible, adaptable, and scalable for businesses of all sizes. From automating repetitive tasks to gaining deeper insights into customer behaviour, AI can help us work smarter, not harder, and improve our bottom line.

When I first started thinking about AI for my business, it felt overwhelming. We didn't know where to begin. My team spent a year experimenting with various tools, from ChatGPT and GitHub Copilot to Figma and Windsurf, and the process was trial and error. But after all the bumps and setbacks, we now have a streamlined AI workflow that's both practical and powerful. I'm here to share that journey with you, to show that AI adoption doesn't have to be a daunting task.

In this chapter, I'll provide a 90-day roadmap for AI adoption that's built around actionable steps and the tools that can accelerate your success. Whether you're just starting or ready to scale, this roadmap will help you navigate the AI landscape.

90-Day AI Adoption Roadmap

This roadmap helped implement AI in our business in just 90 days. It's about getting AI to work for you, step-by-step.

Here's a breakdown of the roadmap:

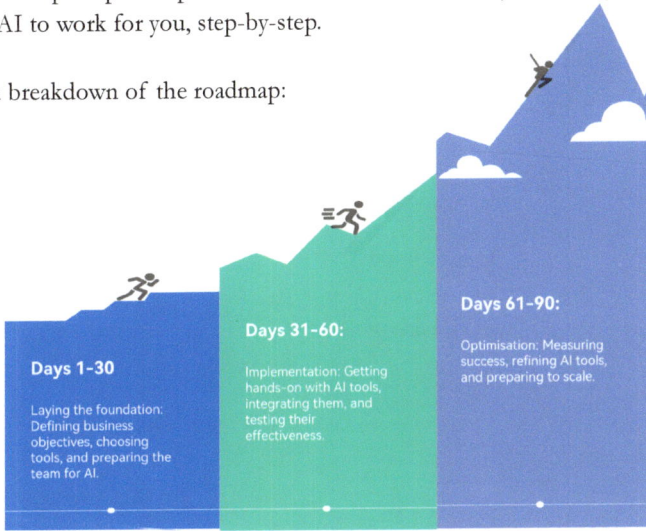

Days 1-30

Laying the foundation: Defining business objectives, choosing tools, and preparing the team for AI.

Days 31-60:

Implementation: Getting hands-on with AI tools, integrating them, and testing their effectiveness.

Days 61-90:

Optimisation: Measuring success, refining AI tools, and preparing to scale.

By the end of these 90 days, our business was AI-enabled, helping us work more efficiently, engage customers better, and grow our business. And it can do the same for you as well.

Day 1-30: Foundation & Initial Setup

The first 30 days are all about setting the foundation. This phase is critical. It's when we define what AI can do for our business, select the right tools, and prepare our team for the transition. These tools will make or break the AI adoption, so choosing the right ones is key.

Let's take a look at the tools we've used at i4T Global and how they fit into this phase.

Define Business Objectives for AI Adoption

When we started our AI journey, the first thing we did was define clear business objectives. AI can do many things, but you need to be specific about what you want to achieve.

Tools used:

- ChatGPT: Initially, we used ChatGPT to help draft business objectives and refine customer engagement strategies. This tool was easy to use and helped generate ideas quickly.

- GitHub Copilot: We also began using GitHub Copilot for some basic automation in the backend. It helped me speed up development tasks by suggesting code, especially in the early stages when I didn't have a developer on hand.

- **Actionable Steps:**

  - We can begin by sitting down with our team and defining 1-3 AI goals we want to achieve, such as improving customer service or automating marketing processes.

  - Use ChatGPT to brainstorm and refine those goals. We can ask it to generate AI-based business strategies or even help you with customer-centric ideas.

  - Make sure these goals are measurable so that we can track progress in the next stages.

Identify High-Impact AI Use Cases

Next, we focused on high-impact AI use cases. We didn't try to do everything at once. Starting small was key.

- **Tools used:**

  - n8n automation: We used n8n to automate repetitive tasks. This was a perfect fit because we could set up workflows with minimal technical knowledge. For example, we set up an automated workflow for lead generation, which integrated email responses into our CRM.

  - Figma: For customer-facing solutions, we used Figma to design AI-driven customer service bots, testing the user interface (UI) for better interaction.

- **Actionable Steps:**

  - We can look at our business goals and choose 1-2 key areas for AI adoption. For me, that was automating customer support and fast-tracking marketing processes.

  - Select tools that will help implement these areas efficiently. For customer support, a tool like ChatGPT can help automate responses to common queries, and n8n can connect various systems to trigger actions (like sending emails or creating tasks).

Select the Right AI Tools & Platforms

I found selecting the right tools a bit challenging at first. There were so many options, and each had different capabilities. But by the end of this phase, I'd selected tools that were easy to implement, yet scalable for future growth.

- **Tools used:**

  - Heygen: We used Heygen to create AI-generated avatars for customer interaction, initially experimenting with basic video creation. The simplicity and low cost of the platform made it a great starting point.

  - Figma: While we didn't use Figma directly for AI at first, we used it for the design aspect, particularly for visualising how AI tools would interact with users.

  - ChatGPT: We used ChatGPT for a multitude of time-consuming tasks, including email campaigns, social media, web copy, image generation, market research, and exploring new ideas.

- **Actionable Steps:**

  - Research AI tools that fit a specific use case. When looking for easy implementation, tools like Heygen or Figma are fantastic for creative tasks, and n8n for backend automation.

  - Choose no-code or low-code platforms so teams can get started quickly without deep technical expertise.

Team Readiness & AI Education

One of the biggest challenges I faced was ensuring my team was ready to embrace AI. Initially, I felt a bit of resistance; people were unsure about how AI would affect their roles. But with the right approach, this became one of the most rewarding parts of the process.

- **Tools used:**

  - GitHub Copilot: We used Copilot not just for development, but to introduce AI coding assistants to my team. We had a workshop on how to use Copilot for faster coding and automating basic tasks.

- Figma: To show the team how AI could work in real-life applications, we ran a collaborative workshop where they designed customer service tools using Figma and Heygen.

- **Actionable Steps:**

  - Appoint an AI champion from the team to lead the effort and answer questions.

  - Get the team started with basic AI training using online resources (e.g., Coursera, LinkedIn Learning).

Use tools like GitHub Copilot to introduce teams to AI-powered workflows in a practical, hands-on way.

Establish Success Metrics

Without clear success metrics, it's impossible to track whether AI is making a difference. We learned this the hard way. The first couple of months felt a bit like "guesswork" until we defined key performance indicators (KPIs).

- **Tools used:**

  - Windsurf: Windsurf became essential for tracking AI performance during our sales and marketing campaigns. It allowed us to set specific KPIs like lead conversion rates and customer satisfaction after interacting with AI tools.

  - n8n automation: For ongoing performance, we used n8n to create automated reports that gathered data on how well AI tools were meeting KPIs.

- **Actionable Steps:**

  - Define measurable KPIs for AI adoption. For example, track improvements in customer satisfaction or sales conversions.

  - Use Windsurf to monitor and assess AI performance, especially for marketing and customer interactions.

  - Set up an automated reporting system using n8n to track and measure results.

Day 31-60: Implementation & Integration

The first 30 days were all about laying the foundation: defining goals, choosing tools, and preparing the team. Now it's time to get hands-on. Days 31-60 are about taking the AI tools you've selected and integrating them into your business. This phase is when you begin to see AI transform from an idea into real-world results.

It's also where I ran into my first real challenges, but with those came some of the best learning moments.

Set Up AI Tools and Integrate with Existing Systems

The first major step in this phase was getting the tools up and running. It wasn't as smooth as I thought it would be. Integrating AI into our existing systems, like CRM, email platforms, and website, was tricky at first. But once we figured out how to make it all work together, the value became clear. We had to test, tweak, and adjust.

The first AI tool we implemented was ChatGPT for automating customer service queries. It took a bit of fine-tuning. At first, the bot didn't always pick up on the nuances of customer questions. But after refining the scripts and feeding them more data, it started to handle 90% of our inbound enquiries efficiently.

Then we integrated GitHub Copilot for code suggestions, which sped up the development of new features for my website. The combination of GitHub Copilot and n8n automation made it possible to link these systems together. n8n automates processes like syncing customer data and leads from the chatbot into our CRM, automatically creating a follow-up task.

- **Actionable Steps:**
  - Start with one pilot project (e.g., add a website chatbot for handling customer inquiries).

- Integrate the new AI tool with CRM, email, and other systems. This ensures seamless data flow between systems (e.g., syncing chatbot interactions with CRM data).

- Test functionality thoroughly: run real-world tests to see if AI is doing what we expect.

Integration is key to making AI tools work within our business infrastructure. This phase isn't just about adding technology; it's about making it function within our ecosystem.

Data Collection & Preparation

Data is the lifeblood of AI. The tools can only be as good as the data they're fed. In this phase, we spent some time cleaning up data and making sure it was structured and ready to be used.

At first, we were a little disorganised with our data. We realised that our customer queries and operational data were scattered across different platforms. Integrating everything into n8n automation helped centralise data flow from multiple systems (email, CRM, website interactions).

We also used Windsurf for tracking the data in real-time, ensuring that the AI tools were getting accurate and up-to-date data.

- **Actionable Steps:**

    - Centralise data across platforms (CRM, customer interactions, emails, etc.).

    - Remove duplicates and ensure it's in a format that AI tools can read easily.

    - Automate data flow between systems, ensuring real-time updates.

Data preparation is everything when it comes to AI. Without clean, structured data, our AI tools won't be able to provide meaningful insights or automate effectively.

Team Collaboration and Cross-Departmental Involvement

We quickly realised that AI adoption isn't something we can do alone. We needed to get everyone on board, especially the teams that would be directly interacting with AI tools. Getting feedback from different departments early on was crucial. We spent a lot of time talking to our customer service team about the AI tools we were testing, specifically the ChatGPT chatbot. They had some valuable feedback on how the bot could be improved, and I realised that AI tools needed to evolve with human input.

- Actionable Steps:

    o Involve all relevant teams early on: engineering, marketing, customer service, sales, etc.

    o Get their input on AI use cases and feedback on how tools are performing.

    o Collaborate with departments to refine and improve AI functionality (e.g., adjusting chatbot scripts based on customer service feedback).

AI adoption is more effective when we collaborate with teams across the business. Cross-department involvement ensures the tools are optimised and accepted by those who will use them the most.

Test and Refine AI Tools

It took time, but by this stage, we were running tests on all the AI tools we had implemented. This was when we started to see the real value of AI. As we fine-tuned the tools based on real-world data, we saw improvements in efficiency and accuracy.

We tested the chatbot on live customer queries and realised it needed some improvements in recognising different customer needs. At first, it could handle only basic questions. However, after tweaking the dialogue and feeding it more examples, it started handling more complex queries too.

- Actionable Steps:
  - Run tests using real customer data and monitor AI's performance.

  - Make adjustments based on feedback. If your chatbot is misbehaving, tweak the dialogue or give it more data to process.

  - Refine predictive models using more structured data to improve accuracy.

AI is a work in progress. The more you test and refine, the more effective it becomes. This iterative process ensures your AI tools are continually improving.

Set Up Reporting and Analytics

Early on, it was hard to know if AI was actually having the desired impact. Once we set up proper reporting and tracking systems, everything changed.

Tracking customer interactions and AI-driven processes allowed us to see real-time performance. We could track response times and measure customer satisfaction. These analytics were a game-changer and helped us make data-driven decisions.

- Actionable Steps:

  - Set up reporting dashboards using tools to track performance.

  - Monitor AI tools regularly for key metrics like customer satisfaction, automation efficiency, and cost savings.

  - Use AI analytics tools to get deeper insights into the effectiveness of the tools.

Tracking performance is the only way to know if AI is delivering on its promises. Without it, we'll be guessing, and miss out on valuable insights for continuous improvement.

Takeaway: The second 30 days are all about getting AI tools up and running and integrating them into our business systems. Yes, there will be challenges, but this is where the real fun begins. By Day 60, you'll have a working AI solution that's ready to be fine-tuned and scaled.

Day 61-90: Optimisation & Early Measurement

By the time we reached Days 61-90, we had made it through the early hurdles. Our AI tools were up and running, and the team was getting comfortable using them. Now, the focus shifted to optimising these tools, tracking their performance, and preparing to scale them across our business.

I remember during this phase, we started seeing the real impact AI could have. It wasn't just about automation or saving time, but about enhancing decision-making, boosting efficiency, and providing me with actionable insights.

But it didn't happen overnight. This phase required a lot of testing, tweaking, and gathering feedback.

Let me walk you through how we approached this and how you can apply the same approach.

Measure Early Success & Gather Feedback

At this point, it's vital to assess whether the AI tools are achieving our goals. I remember feeling a mix of excitement and nervousness as we started measuring real outcomes. We wanted to make sure AI was actually making a difference, was it improving response times, pushing better content at scale, or reducing manual effort?

Early on, we tracked key metrics such as customer satisfaction, time saved, and cost reduction. The results weren't always perfect. For example, our chatbot needed refinement to handle more complex queries. But this feedback was crucial. It allowed us to pinpoint where the chatbot was falling short and make adjustments.

- Actionable Steps:

    o Track key performance indicators (KPIs). For example, if we're using a chatbot, we need to monitor response times, customer satisfaction, and problem resolution rates.

    o Gather feedback from the team and customers. Ask employees how AI is improving their workflow and whether customers are satisfied with AI-driven interactions.

o Measure engagement with AI tools (e.g., how often customers interact with the chatbot or how accurate our sales forecasts are).

Measuring success at this stage helps us understand whether the AI tools are having the desired impact. It's important to catch any issues early, so we can tweak and improve before scaling.

Iterate Based on Feedback

We quickly realised that AI tools are rarely perfect right out of the box. But the good news? Iteration is how AI improves.

After gathering the initial feedback, we spent a lot of time refining our tools. Whether it was fine-tuning the chatbot's scripts or adjusting marketing processes, it was a continuous process of tweaking and improving.

For example, the chatbot was great for basic questions, but when it came to more specific customer enquiries, it fell short. We made updates by feeding it more customer data, refining responses, and even retraining parts of the system. The results were noticeable. Customer satisfaction improved, and we started saving more time on repetitive tasks.

- Actionable Steps:

    o Review feedback regularly to identify areas for improvement.

    o Make small adjustments to refine the AI tool. For example, improve chatbot responses, tweak predictive models, or adjust automation processes.

    o Test changes and measure the impact to see if the adjustments lead to improvements.

AI systems get better over time. Continuous improvement means your tools will evolve and deliver even more value as you fine-tune them.

Document Learnings & Prepare for Scaling

At this point, we had learned a lot about what works and what doesn't.

For us, documenting these insights was one of the most important parts of the process. It wasn't just about what AI could do now; it was about planning for the next phase and how we could scale these AI tools across different areas of the business.

111

We spent time documenting the lessons learned from the pilot phase. This gave us a clearer idea of how we could expand AI to other functions. We also used the feedback from the first 60 days to create a roadmap for scaling AI tools to the rest of the business.

- Actionable Steps:

    o Ask what worked well? What didn't? Documenting this helps you avoid mistakes when you scale AI to other areas.

    o Identify other areas in the business that can benefit from AI, like sales, marketing, or operations.

    o Create a scaling plan for how AI can be extended to more departments and business functions.

Scaling AI beyond the pilot phase requires careful planning. By documenting our learnings and preparing for growth, we set ourselves up for long-term success.

Refine AI Strategies for Long-Term Growth

Once AI is up and running, we've got to think beyond the initial phase.

The tools we implemented in the first 60 days are just the beginning. In this phase, it's important to ensure that our AI strategy is flexible and can evolve with our business.

Over the first 90 days, we had to adapt our strategy based on what we learned. Initially, we focused mostly on customer service automation. As AI proved its value, we expanded it to marketing automation and product development as well. This required updating our overall AI strategy to align with new business goals.

- Actionable Steps:

    o Review the AI strategy. Is it still aligned with the long-term business objectives? If goals have shifted, adapt the AI strategy accordingly.

    o As AI tools evolve, invest in regular training to ensure teams stay up to date with the latest developments.

    o AI is evolving rapidly, and staying on top of new tools and innovations will keep your business competitive.

Long-term growth with AI requires an evolving strategy. By regularly reviewing and refining our AI approach, we ensured that it continues to support business goals and adapt to new opportunities.

Takeaway: Optimisation is the stage where the real impact of AI starts to show, and it's where you can take your tools from basic automation to true business transformation.

Moving Beyond Day 90

Congratulations! You've completed your 90-day AI adoption roadmap!

By now, we've laid a solid foundation, integrated AI tools into our business, and optimised them for performance. But the journey doesn't end here.

AI adoption is a continuous process. The next step is scaling AI throughout your business and maintaining its growth as technology evolves.

Here are a few things we learned along the way, and you need to remember to keep the momentum going and ensure your AI strategy continues to deliver long-term value.

AI Adoption is Ongoing

Even after the 90-day mark, our business must continue to evolve and adapt. AI technologies improve over time, so you should be prepared to iterate, optimise, and scale as our business grows. Don't consider this a one-off project; think of it as part of your long-term strategy.

Scale AI Across the Business

By the end of the 90 days, one should have one or two AI tools up and running. Now it's time to expand and scale. Identify additional areas of your business that could benefit from AI tools and integrate them into existing processes.

Expand AI use cases to other departments, automate more tasks, and integrate more data sources.

Keep Measuring & Optimising

Just because our AI tools are working doesn't mean the work is done. The key to sustained success is constant optimisation. Regularly measure performance, gather feedback, and adjust AI tools based on what's working and what needs improvement.

Set up monthly reviews, solicit team feedback, and refine models. This ensures that AI tools are always improving and that our business stays ahead of the curve, driving long-term value.

Stay Focused on the Bigger Picture

AI is powerful, but it's just one piece of your digital transformation puzzle.

As we scale AI in our business, we need to make sure it stays aligned with our broader goals. We must keep AI integrated into our overall business strategy and balance AI with human creativity.

This marks the end of our 90-day roadmap, but our AI adoption doesn't stop here. At i4T Global, we keep refining, expanding, and measuring the impact of AI to unlock even greater value for ourselves and our SME clients as their trusted IT consultant.

Chapter 09:

Top Tools for SMEs in 2026 and Beyond

As we look towards 2026, the way we do business is changing fast.

AI-powered tools, low-code platforms, and automation aren't just for the big players anymore; they're here for everyone. Whether we're running a start-up or a growing SME, these tools are making it easier than ever to work smarter, not harder, and stay ahead of the game.

But with so many options out there, it's easy to feel overwhelmed. This chapter will help us cut through the noise.

Together, we'll walk through the top tools that are already transforming how small businesses operate. From marketing to operations, CRM to analytics, these tools will help us streamline tasks, engage customers, and make better decisions, all without needing to be a tech expert.

We already know that digital transformation is about more than just tech. It's about adopting the right mindset, making strategic moves, and building a culture that thrives in the digital world. The tools we'll cover here are the key to making all that happen.

Ready to level up? Let's dive in and explore how these platforms can set our business up for success in the years to come.

Marketing Tools for 2026

In the fast-paced world of marketing, businesses need to be smarter and faster than ever before. Enter AI-powered tools, the game-changers that are revolutionising how companies engage with their customers, boost campaigns, and deliver personalised experiences. By harnessing the power of AI, businesses can make data-driven decisions that elevate their marketing efforts to a whole new level.

Let's explore some of the most exciting tools that will shape marketing towards 2026.

ChatGPT for Content Creation and Customer Engagement

ChatGPT is transforming the way businesses create content and interact with customers. It's an AI tool that generates natural language responses for emails, social media posts, and customer queries. Whether you're crafting an engaging blog post or answering customer questions, ChatGPT can automate the entire process, saving time and effort.

Pros:

- Quick content generation: No more hours spent brainstorming ideas or drafting responses. ChatGPT can churn out content in seconds, helping businesses keep up with the demand for fresh, relevant content.

- Scalable customer engagement: ChatGPT can handle multiple customer queries simultaneously, making it perfect for businesses looking to engage with thousands of customers at once.

- 24/7 availability: Since it's AI-driven, it's always on, allowing businesses to maintain constant communication with customers across time zones.

Cons:

- Needs fine-tuning: While ChatGPT can handle a variety of tasks, it may require some tweaking to ensure that the tone, style, and context are just right.

- Content personalisation: ChatGPT is great at creating generic content, but for highly personalised communication, some additional customisation is needed.

Use case: Automating email campaigns, handling customer service queries, and generating social media content. This means our teams can focus on more strategic tasks while the AI takes care of the day-to-day content creation and customer engagement.

Starting with ChatGPT

A Company Guide to Adoption

1. Define Use-Cases

Start small: emails, meeting notes, reports.

2. Assign AI Champions

A few team members to test and share learnings.

3. Set Privacy Guidelines

Don't paste confidential data. Use anonymised info. Consider enterprise ChatGPT for sensitive tasks.

4. Experiment & Iterate

Try prompts, refine, and capture best practices.

5. Create Prompt Library

Save prompts that work best for repeat use.

6. Integrate with Workflows

Connect with CRM, docs, or project tools.

7. Train Staff

Short workshops so everyone feels confident using AI.

8. Review & Measure

Track efficiency gains, adjust strategy, expand use.

Heygen for AI-Generated Video Content

Heygen uses AI to create personalised video content. Video is one of the most engaging forms of content, and Heygen allows businesses to produce dynamic, interactive videos that can be used in a variety of marketing campaigns. From product demos to customer testimonials, this tool brings our content to life in a way that resonates with our audience.

Pros:

- Fast video generation: In a world where content is king, Heygen creates high-quality videos in no time, ideal for fast-moving marketing campaigns.

- Low technical barriers: Unlike traditional video editing tools that require specialized knowledge, Heygen's user-friendly interface makes it easy for anyone to create professional-looking videos.

- Highly customisable: Want to add a brand logo, change the background, or tweak the message? Heygen offers plenty of customisation options.

Cons:

Limited depth for highly professional video production: While Heygen excels at creating quick, personalised videos, it may not be suited for highly polished, complex video projects that require a professional touch.

Use case: Creating personalised video ads, promotional videos, and educational content for customers. It's an easy way to engage your audience, boost brand awareness, and drive conversions, all without the need for a full-scale video production team.

Figma for AI-Enhanced Design

Figma is a collaborative design tool that integrates AI to streamline the creation of websites and marketing materials. Whether you're designing landing pages, social media ads, or user interfaces, Figma's AI-driven templates and features make the design process faster, smarter, and more collaborative than ever before.

Pros:

- Intuitive interface: Figma is known for its easy-to-use design interface that helps both designers and non-designers create stunning visuals.

- Collaborative features: Multiple team members can work on a design in real time, making collaboration a breeze, even for remote teams.

- Cloud-based: Being cloud-based means that anyone can access and update designs from anywhere, ensuring our teams are always on the same page.

Cons:

Limited functionality for complex animations: While Figma is excellent for static and simple designs, it may not be the best tool for more intricate animations or interactive features that require advanced design software.

Use case: Creating personalised video ads, promotional videos, and educational content for customers. It's an easy way to engage your audience, boost brand awareness, and drive conversions, all without the need for a full-scale video production team.

Streamlining Operations with AI

AI is no longer just something we hear about in customer service or marketing; it's now making a huge impact on the back-end of businesses as well.

From automating repetitive tasks to supercharging team collaboration, AI tools are helping businesses become faster, smarter, and more efficient.

Let's take a look at some of the AI-powered tools that are transforming how we work behind the scenes.

n8n for Workflow Automation

Imagine one could take all those time-consuming, repetitive tasks off your plate, automatically. That's exactly what n8n does. This AI tool allows you to connect different apps and systems, creating seamless workflows that run themselves. Whether it's syncing customer data, managing approvals, or automating daily reports, n8n is there to make our business operations smoother and quicker.

Pros:

- Highly customisable: n8n lets us create workflows tailored to your business. No need to settle for pre-set solutions; we can build exactly what we need.

- No-code: We don't need to be a coding pro to use n8n. Its intuitive, drag-and-drop interface means anyone can automate processes without technical skills.

- Integrates with hundreds of apps: From Google Sheets to Salesforce, n8n connects with a wide range of apps, letting us automate across our entire tech ecosystem.

Cons:

Learning curve: While it's easy to start, n8n can get a little tricky when we want to design more complex workflows. But once we get the hang of it, the sky's the limit.

Use case: Imagine automatically syncing customer data between our CRM and marketing tools, or triggering an action like sending a thank-you email whenever a new lead signs up. With n8n, we can automate these tasks and free up our team to focus on more meaningful work.

Cursor for Knowledge Management

Cursor is like a digital filing cabinet, but with superpowers. This AI-powered tool organises the company's knowledge, making it easy to store, manage, and find the information a team needs.

Whether it's a document, a report, or a process, Cursor ensures everything is centralised and easily accessible.

Pros:

- Easy access to company knowledge: No more hunting down files. Cursor allows teams to find the information they need in seconds, keeping things moving without a hitch.

- Reduces search time: The days of wasting time searching for documents are over. Cursor speeds up the process, boosting productivity and helping teams work smarter.

- Boosts productivity: With everything at their fingertips, employees can spend more time focusing on delivering value rather than searching for info.

Cons:

Too simplistic for complex knowledge structures: For companies with particularly complex knowledge base, Cursor might feel a bit too simple. It's fantastic for straightforward information, but more intricate systems might need something a little more advanced.

Use case: Think of Cursor as your company's personal assistant, organising everything from internal processes to customer FAQs. It's perfect for making sure teams can quickly access the right information, whenever they need it.

CRM Tools for 2026

When it comes to building lasting customer relationships, a strong Customer Relationship Management (CRM) system is essential.

In 2025, AI-powered CRMs are taking customer engagement to the next level, offering smarter insights, personalised experiences, and seamless automation. These tools are enabling businesses to not only understand their customers better but also engage with them in more meaningful ways.

Let's dive into some of the CRM tools that are revolutionising the way we manage customer relationships.

HubSpot for AI-Driven CRM

HubSpot is a leading CRM platform that leverages AI to help businesses attract, engage, and delight customers. With its AI-driven tools, HubSpot automates many aspects of the customer journey, from lead nurturing to personalised follow-ups, helping businesses stay in touch with their customers without the extra manual effort. It also offers powerful analytics to track customer interactions and improve your engagement strategies.

Pros:

- All-in-one CRM platform: HubSpot brings everything into one place, marketing, sales, customer service, and CRM, making it easy to manage and track customer relationships.

- AI-driven insights: HubSpot's AI tools provide deep insights into customer behaviour, helping businesses make data-backed decisions that improve customer experiences.

- Easy to use: Its intuitive interface makes it simple for teams to get started, even if they don't have a technical background.

Cons:

- It can get expensive as companies scale: While HubSpot offers a free version, some of its advanced features, especially for larger teams, can come with a hefty price tag.

- May require additional integration: For businesses with complex workflows or multiple platforms, integrating HubSpot with other tools might be necessary, adding to the setup time.

Use case: HubSpot is perfect for businesses looking to automate lead nurturing, send personalised emails at scale, and track customer engagement across various touchpoints. With its AI-powered insights, tailoring marketing efforts and improving conversions is easy, all while keeping customer service and sales teams aligned.

Zoho Analytics for Automated Customer Insights

Zoho Analytics is an AI-powered business intelligence and analytics platform that helps companies turn raw data into actionable insights. It automatically analyses customer data, revealing patterns in behaviour, preferences, and purchase trends. This makes it an essential tool for businesses aiming to better understand their audience and fine-tune marketing and sales strategies using real, data-driven insights.

Pros:

- AI-driven insights: Zoho Analytics uses AI and machine learning to identify customer trends, segment audiences, and predict future behaviours, helping businesses tailor their marketing with precision.

- Intuitive interface: The platform is designed for ease of use, offering drag-and-drop dashboards and visual reports that make analytics accessible to non-technical users.

- Real-time analytics: With live data syncing, Zoho Analytics enables teams to respond quickly to changing customer behaviour and market conditions.

- Customisable reports: Businesses can build dashboards that highlight exactly what matters most, whether it's campaign performance, sales trends, or customer retention metrics.

Cons:

- Complex setup for large datasets: For businesses managing vast amounts of data, initial configuration and integration can require time and expertise.

- Integration dependency: While Zoho integrates with hundreds of apps, accessing advanced features may depend on other Zoho ecosystem tools or paid add-ons.

Use Case: Zoho Analytics is ideal for businesses looking to elevate their customer understanding and sharpen marketing precision. By automatically segmenting customers based on demographics, behaviour, and purchase history, companies can personalise campaigns, improve targeting, and enhance overall customer engagement. For small to medium-sized businesses, it offers a cost-effective way to harness the power of data without the need for a dedicated analytics team.

Bringing it Together

Every industry has its own unique needs. While one CRM might fit us as a technology vendor, the clients we served had their own very different needs.

This led us to work on a purpose-built CRM solution for one of our Field Service clients.

i4T CRM, as we call it, offers all essential customer relationship management features that small to medium businesses can benefit from, including: Leads and Sales Management, Customer and Contact Management, Marketing, Campaign and Analytics, to name a few.

We also powered it with AI capabilities such as automatically creating lead titles where missing by pulling in and analysing details of a particular contact.

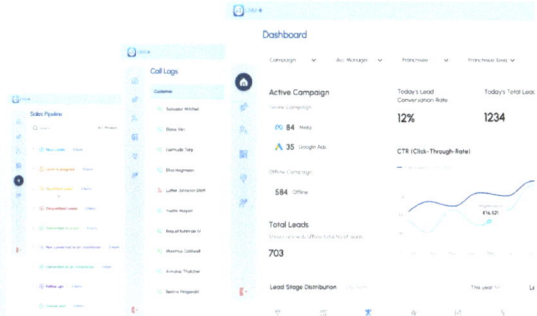

CRM X FSM

Built for Field Service Suppliers Who Want to Close Deals and Deliver on Them

Bridge the gap between sales and operations. Manage leads, convert them into jobs, and track service delivery, all from one place.

Analytics Tools for 2026

In today's fast-paced digital landscape, data-driven decision-making is more crucial than ever.

With the rise of AI-powered analytics tools, businesses can now track, interpret, and act on data with incredible ease and precision.

These tools are not only helping companies stay on top of trends but are also empowering them to make smarter, more informed decisions.

Let's dive into two of the leading AI-powered analytics tools that are reshaping how businesses harness data.

Google Analytics 4 with AI Integration

Google Analytics 4 (GA4) takes data analysis to the next level by integrating AI and machine learning to provide deeper insights into customer behaviour, trends, and conversion rates. Unlike its predecessor, GA4 is designed to deliver more predictive insights, allowing businesses to anticipate user actions and make real-time adjustments to their strategies. It tracks everything from website performance to customer journeys, helping businesses optimise every part of their marketing funnel.

Pros:

- Predictive insights: GA4 uses AI to forecast user behaviour, such as the likelihood of conversions, allowing businesses to take proactive measures rather than reacting after the fact.

- User-friendly: The platform is designed to be intuitive, with a clear interface that simplifies the complex process of tracking and analysing data.

- Seamless integration: GA4 integrates smoothly with other Google tools like Google Ads and Google Tag Manager, giving you a unified view of a business's marketing efforts.

Cons:

- Steep learning curve: For newcomers, GA4 can feel overwhelming due to its new structure and advanced features.

- Complex setup for advanced features: While the basic setup is straightforward, using GA4's advanced machine learning capabilities requires a bit of technical know-how and configuration.

Use case: Tracking website performance, understanding user behaviour, and measuring campaign success. With GA4, businesses can analyse how users interact with their website, predict future actions, and adjust their marketing strategies accordingly. It's perfect for businesses looking to gain deeper insights into customer journeys and improve conversion rates.

Tableau for Data Visualisation and Analytics

Tableau is an advanced analytics tool that leverages AI to provide powerful data visualisation and business intelligence capabilities. It helps businesses transform complex data into interactive, visual insights that are easy to understand and act upon.

Whether we're tracking KPIs, analysing trends, or creating detailed reports, Tableau's AI-driven features turn raw data into actionable insights that can drive business decisions.

Pros:

- Powerful data visualisation: Tableau excels in transforming data into easy-to-read charts, graphs, and interactive dashboards, making it easier to spot trends and make informed decisions.

- Customisable reports: We can create tailor-made reports that focus on the specific data points most important to your business.

- Real-time analytics: Tableau provides real-time data updates, allowing businesses to track their performance and make decisions based on the latest available information.

Cons:

- High cost: Tableau's pricing can be a barrier for small businesses, as it's typically more expensive than other analytics platforms.

Requires training: To truly harness the power of Tableau, some training is necessary to understand how to use its advanced features and create custom visualisations.

Use case: Building custom dashboards, tracking KPIs, and generating actionable insights from business data. Whether we're looking to track sales performance, monitor website traffic, or analyse customer behaviour, Tableau provides the tools to create powerful, easy-to-understand visual reports that help drive business strategy.

Low-Code & No-Code Platforms for 2026

The rise of low-code and no-code platforms has opened up new doors for businesses to innovate, automate, and scale operations without needing a team of developers.

These platforms allow teams to create powerful tools, websites, and workflows, all while bypassing the complexity of traditional coding.

These user-friendly solutions are empowering businesses to move faster, make smarter decisions, and keep up with the fast-paced digital world.

Let's explore two of the most popular platforms that are revolutionising how businesses operate.

Webflow for Low-Code Web Design

Webflow is a low-code platform that allows businesses to create stunning, responsive websites and custom landing pages without needing to write a single line of code. With a simple drag-and-drop interface,

Webflow lets small businesses design and publish beautiful websites quickly, whether it's launching a product, building a portfolio, or creating a landing page for a campaign.

Pros:

- Easy to use: Webflow's intuitive interface makes web design accessible to non-technical users. It's perfect for businesses that want to create professional websites without relying on developers.

- SEO-friendly: Webflow offers built-in tools that help optimise websites for search engines, ensuring they rank well and attract organic traffic.

- Highly customisable: While it's easy to use, Webflow also allows for a high degree of customisation, so we can design websites and landing pages that perfectly align with our brand.

Cons:

- Limited for complex web applications: Webflow is fantastic for websites and landing pages, but might not be the best fit for more complex web applications or custom features that require advanced coding.

Use case: Webflow is ideal for businesses looking to build websites and landing pages quickly, using AI-powered templates that help get started. It's a great tool for creating responsive, attractive pages that work seamlessly across devices, without the need for a developer.

Zapier for Workflow Automation

Zapier connects hundreds of apps and automates workflows, allowing businesses to automate repetitive tasks without any coding. From syncing data between apps to automating lead capture or managing customer support tickets, Zapier integrates with your existing tools and streamlines your processes, freeing up time for more important work.

Pros:
- No-code automation: With Zapier, anyone can automate workflows without needing technical skills. We simply select the apps we want to connect, set the triggers and actions, and let Zapier take care of the rest.

- Seamless integrations: Zapier connects with over 2,000 apps, including popular platforms like Google Sheets, Slack, and Salesforce, allowing SMEs to automate a wide range of processes.

- Time-saving: By automating repetitive tasks, Zapier helps save time and reduce the risk of human error in workflows.

Cons:
- Limited advanced features for large enterprises: While Zapier is great for small businesses and SMEs, it might fall short for larger enterprises with more complex automation needs. Advanced functionality can sometimes require a more robust solution.

How AI Levels the Playing Field for SMBs

Work order in progress   20%

Door Lock Repair

Active Campaign
∞ 84 Meta

Compliant

The i4T Global Story

i4T Global is a dynamic technology company focused on delivering cutting-edge solutions in the PropTech and Field Service Management sectors. Its competitive edge lay not just in innovative solutions but in superior customer support, being an easy-to-approach company, and a laser-sharp customer focus.

The Challenge

As operations grew, so did the customers' demands. Despite having the technical expertise, the small team lacked the resources to scale quickly, automate tasks, and keep up with the rapidly evolving market demands. Efficiency and customer engagement were critical pain points. i4T Global needed to automate repetitive tasks, improve internal collaboration, generate high-quality content at scale, and transform customer data into actionable insights.

The Solution: AI Integration

New feature requests, more support tickets, and bigger marketing initiatives meant just one thing: If it were to provide the same level of service to its clients, without adding more heads to the team, i4T Global needed to revisit its processes. **AI was the natural answer.**

The AI-Powered Toolkit

Content Creation & Engagement
Tool: ChatGPT

Automated content creation for blogs, social media, and customer interactions, enabling i4T Global to scale engagement without sacrificing quality. This allowed the team to focus on strategic initiatives, helping the business compete with larger players while maintaining personalised communication.

Dynamic Video Content
Tool: Heygen

Heygen allowed i4T Global's marketing team to quickly create personalised, high-quality video content, driving customer interaction and increasing conversion rates. With video being key to modern marketing, this tool helped the business match the content output of much larger organisations.

Design Optimisation
Tool: Figma

Figma streamlined the UI/UX design process using AI-powered templates, allowing i4T Global to rapidly prototype responsive, SEO-friendly websites and landing pages. This helped the team launch campaigns faster and maintain brand consistency across platforms.

Workflow Automation
Tool: n8n

n8n automated i4T Global's marketing, sales, and admin tasks, reducing manual work and saving time. It connected multiple apps to streamline data syncing, lead management, and customer communications, allowing the team to focus on high-priority activities.

Coding & Unit Testing
Tools: GitHub Copilot, Windsurf, Cursor

GitHub Copilot sped up development by suggesting code, while Windsurf efficiently handled unit testing. Cursor improved knowledge management for coding, making resources more accessible and increasing developer productivity.

Quality Assurance
Tool: Katlan Studio

Katlan Studio automated the development team's QA processes, providing insights into potential issues and speeding up testing. This allowed the team to deliver high-quality products faster, enhancing reliability and improving client satisfaction.

The Results

The integration of these AI-powered tools not only helped i4T Global streamline operations and improve team collaboration but also allowed it to deliver better results to clients. By automating repetitive tasks, creating personalised content, and leveraging data-driven insights, i4T Global positioned itself as a more agile, efficient, and customer-centric business. These tools are now at the core of its operations, enabling the company to scale quickly, innovate continuously, and maintain a competitive edge.

130

Tools for a Future-Ready Business

As we look ahead to 2026 and beyond, the tools covered in this chapter, and many more mentioned in the "Top 50 AI Tools for Businesses with a Small Budget", provided in the appendix, are set to transform how businesses operate. From AI-driven customer engagement to workflow automation and data analytics, the tools we've explored will help businesses work smarter, not harder. Whether we're just starting our digital transformation or scaling our AI efforts, these tools are essential for future-proofing our business and staying competitive in the ever-evolving landscape.

Chapter 10:

Case Studies - Lessons from the Frontlines

One truth about digital and AI transformation is that it never follows a neat textbook script.

We've spent the past chapters exploring the big ideas: why our business must think digital first, how to build a human-centric culture, and how to start small and scale from there.

But the moment we set foot on the ground, we will realise real change is messy.

It's driven by ambition, powered by people, and tested by every hiccup, obstacle, and curveball one can imagine.

Plans get rewritten and budgets stretch. Sometimes we launch something brilliant, and it flops. Other times, a pilot we half-expected to fail becomes the breakthrough that transforms our whole business.

So in this chapter, we are diving into the frontlines: SMEs who took the plunge and ultimately how each found its way forward.

Because at the end of the day, it's not the perfect roadmaps that drive real transformation. It's the grit, resilience, and willingness to learn by doing.

Ballarat Solar Company (Australia)

With the boom in solar installations across Australia, one small solar company was struggling to keep up with incoming customer calls. Every day, their phone lines were flooded with enquiries, some from new leads curious about solar systems, others from existing customers chasing updates or service requests. The team found themselves overwhelmed, and the manual call handling process was inconsistent and error-prone. That's when they approached i4T Global to design an AI-powered call assistant tailored specifically for the solar industry.

The Challenge

The solar company's staff were spending too much time on repetitive intake calls, while more complex sales conversations were being delayed. Missed follow-ups meant lost business. The business needed a solution that could:

- Answer incoming calls reliably,

- Identify whether the caller was a lead or existing customer,

- Capture relevant information automatically, and

- Integrate seamlessly with their CRM.

But there was no ready-made AI solution available for the solar industry. The path forward was uncertain.

The Solution

i4T Global built a domain-specific AI call assistant, trained on solar knowledge and customer scenarios. The assistant could answer questions in natural conversation, extract details about the caller's needs, and record everything directly into the CRM. Features included:

- A voice assistant tailored to solar terminology,

- Custom speech analysis and data extraction,

- Intelligent fallback to human agents,

- Continuous fine-tuning of voice and scenarios,

- Porting of existing customer phone numbers into the AI system.

What Worked

- Automation of intake: The AI reduced the load on staff by handling common enquiries and initial data capture.

- CRM integration: Every call was logged with accurate customer details, ensuring no lead slipped through the cracks.

- Improved response times: With the AI covering first-line calls, the sales team could focus on high-value conversations.

What Didn't Work

- Some customers resisted speaking to an AI and insisted on a human.

- The CRM integration needed custom development.

- The AI required extensive fine-tuning to handle the variety of customer questions.

Mid-journey Pivot

To address these challenges, the company:
- Added clear handover options to human staff for customers who didn't want AI.

- Developed tighter integrations with the CRM to improve data accuracy.

- Continuously refined the assistant using real call recordings, making it sound more natural and aligned with the company's brand voice.

Results
- The AI now handles the majority of intake calls, eliminating call center costs.

- Customer wait times dropped significantly, improving satisfaction.

- The business gained better data on customer enquiries, helping the sales team follow up faster and close more deals.

- From the first call to quoting, the entire workflow was automated.

Amarra (New Jersey, USA)

Amarra is a wholesale distributor that specialises in special-occasion gowns, catering to both retail and online businesses. The company supplies dresses for weddings, proms, and other formal events. In a bid to improve operational efficiency, customer experience, and digital presence, Amarra turned to AI-powered solutions. [10]

The Challenge

Amarra struggled with the large volume of customer inquiries, the time-consuming task of writing product descriptions, and managing inventory across multiple platforms. The manual effort involved in drafting product descriptions and handling customer queries was draining resources and slowing down operations.

The Solution

To tackle these challenges, Amarra introduced AI-driven content generation tools to automate product descriptions and AI chatbots to manage customer queries. They also deployed AI-powered inventory forecasting tools that analysed sales trends, seasonality, and other influencing factors to predict demand for different gowns.

What Worked

- Content creation: The AI tool reduced the time required to create product descriptions significantly, improving consistency and speed across product listings.

- AI chatbots: By handling most of customer inquiries, the chatbots freed up staff to focus on more complex tasks.

- Demand forecasting: AI-driven forecasts improved inventory management, ensuring stock levels were aligned with demand and reducing overstock.

What Didn't Work

- Chatbot tone: Initially, the chatbots' responses were perceived as too robotic, which led to customer complaints about a lack of personalisation.

- Data quality: The AI models used for inventory forecasting were initially hindered by inconsistent or low-quality data from suppliers, which affected prediction accuracy.

Mid-journey Pivot

- Amarra fine-tuned the chatbot's tone by incorporating more human-like responses and involved staff in reviewing chatbot interactions to ensure the brand voice was maintained.

- They implemented a data-cleaning process for inventory and began testing AI predictions on a smaller subset of products before scaling.

Results

- The AI-generated content reduced the time spent on product listings by 60%.

- The chatbots successfully managed 70% of customer interactions, improving response times and allowing human staff to focus on more complex issues.

Inventory waste was reduced, and Amarra saw more accurate stock management thanks to the improved AI forecasting.

Restoke (Melbourne, Australia)

Restoke is a Melbourne-based AI startup focused on optimising restaurant inventory and reducing food waste. The company uses AI to help restaurants manage their stock, predict demand, and minimise wastage. Their goal is to streamline restaurant operations and maximise profitability. [11]

The Challenge

The restaurant industry is notorious for difficulties in demand prediction, often leading to overordering or underordering ingredients. This problem is compounded by a lack of systems that track stock levels and consumption patterns accurately, resulting in either waste or missed revenue opportunities.

The Solution

Restoke implemented an AI-powered inventory management system that integrates with POS and inventory systems. The platform uses real-time sales and order data to forecast ingredient demand and recommend purchase orders. Additionally, historical consumption data is analysed to keep stock levels optimised.

What Worked

- Inventory Management: The AI-driven system improved stock accuracy, reducing food waste by 30% and ensuring stock levels were always optimal.

- Cost Savings: Restaurants reported savings of up to AU$8,000 per week thanks to better demand prediction and reduced waste.

What Didn't Work

- **Resistance to AI:** Some restaurant managers were reluctant to trust AI systems over their traditional methods, particularly in smaller, more established venues.

- **Integration issues:** The platform's integration with legacy POS systems posed challenges in older venues, where outdated technology wasn't always compatible with the new system.

Mid-journey Pivot

- Restoke provided training modules to help restaurant owners and staff understand the value of the system and increase adoption rates.

- They worked closely with smaller venues to simplify integrations and ensure the platform was user-friendly for businesses with less technical infrastructure.

The Results

- Restaurants using Restoke saved AU$8,000 per week on average by improving stock management.

- The system expanded to 2,000+ venues globally, and real-time stock forecasting has become a cornerstone of daily operations.

- Operational efficiency improved, with staff spending less time manually tracking and ordering stock.

The Original Tamale Company (Viral Marketing with AI)

The Original Tamale Company is a family-owned eatery based in Pacoima, Los Angeles, renowned for its delicious, handcrafted tamales. Established with a focus on authentic flavours and high-quality ingredients, the restaurant has become a local favourite. [11]

The Challenge

As a small, family-run business with limited marketing resources, The Original Tamale Company faced the challenge of increasing visibility and attracting new customers in a competitive market.

The Solution

Christian Ortega, the owner's nephew and head of marketing, utilised ChatGPT to script a humorous 46-second video. The video depicted a man falling from an aeroplane, with a narrator offering quirky advice, ultimately suggesting landing at the tamale shop. The AI-generated script was paired with a voiceover and visual content, creating a meme-inspired, engaging advertisement.

What Worked

- Rapid Production: The video was created in just 10 minutes, allowing for timely engagement with trending content.

- Viral Engagement: The video garnered over 22 million views and 1.2 million likes within three weeks, significantly boosting the restaurant's online presence.

- Celebrity Endorsement: The video attracted attention from celebrities, including sports analyst Emmanuel Acho and actor Peter Gadiot, amplifying its reach.

- Increased Foot Traffic: Customers reported visiting the restaurant after seeing the video, citing its humour and positive reviews as motivating factors.

What Didn't Work

- Initial Skepticism: There was initial hesitation about relying on AI for creative content, with concerns about maintaining authenticity and brand voice.

- Over-reliance on Trends: The success was partly due to capitalising on a viral meme, which may not be sustainable long-term.

Mid-journey Pivot

- Recognising the importance of balancing AI-generated content with authentic brand messaging, Ortega continued to use AI as a tool while ensuring that the content resonated with the restaurant's identity and values.

The Results

- Significant Increase in Followers: The restaurant's social media following grew substantially following the video's release.

- Enhanced Brand Recognition: The viral video established The Original Tamale Company as a creative and engaging brand in the local food scene.

- Boosted Sales: The influx of new customers and heightened brand awareness contributed to increased sales and business growth.

Key Takeaways for Small Businesses Using AI

AI isn't just a buzzword; it's a powerful tool that can change the way small businesses operate, interact with customers, and optimise internal processes.

From handling customer calls in the Australian solar industry to improving customer engagement at Amarra, reducing food waste with Restoke, and boosting engagement on The Original Tamale Company, the message is clear: AI's value is unlocked when businesses pair the right tools with the right mindset.

Invest in People as Much as Technology

AI might be a technological marvel, but its effectiveness truly depends on the people using it.

- The solar installer's AI call assistant only worked once staff embraced it as a partner, not a replacement.

- Amarra and Restoke also found that training and cultural adoption were just as critical as the technology itself.

- The Original Tamale Company leveraged the attention they got from celebrities.

What to take away

Our team needs to be tech-savvy and open to learning. It's not just about installing AI tools; it's about getting people on board with change management and ensuring the human element continues to complement and optimise the AI system.

Data Quality and Accuracy Are Crucial

Whether it's call logs in a solar CRM, inventory at Restoke, or herd data on Israeli farms, clean and structured data is the foundation for meaningful AI insights. In all these cases, poor or incomplete data held back results until businesses improved their collection and cleansing processes.

What to take away

Clean data is the foundation for successful AI. Businesses should focus on data management, whether sales, customer interactions, or product performance. Without structured and accurate data, AI tools will struggle to provide meaningful insights.

Personalisation Is a Key Driver of Engagement

Customers want personal experiences that speak to their individual needs.

- The solar company improved customer trust once its AI sounded more natural and aligned with its brand.

- Amarra's chatbot delivered tailored product recommendations.

- Restoke suggested personalised menu items based on order history.

What to take away

Personalisation is key. AI can help us deliver hyper-relevant experiences that not only engage customers but also foster loyalty. Whether through customised offers, recommendations, or personalised services, AI allows us to go the extra mile for our customers and make them feel seen and valued.

Start Small, Scale Gradually

No one succeeds by going "all in" on day one.
- The solar installer started by automating only intake calls before expanding the assistant's scope.

- Restoke rolled out AI inventory systems in pilot venues before scaling.

- Amarra gradually introduced AI-driven content and chatbots.

What to take away

From handling customer calls in the Australian solar industry to improving customer engagement at Amarra, reducing food waste with Restoke, and boosting engagement on The Original Tamale Company, the message is clear: AI's value is unlocked when businesses pair the right tools with the right mindset

Embrace the Learning Curve

AI is never "done."

- The solar installer kept refining its AI with real call recordings.

- The Original Tamale Company balanced AI-generated content with authentic brand messaging

- Amarra and Restoke tweaked their models to better predict demand.

What to take away

AI is always evolving. Small businesses should invest not only in initial setup but also in ongoing learning and adaptation. Ensure that systems are constantly evolving to reflect changes in data, the market, and customer needs.

Put these lessons into action and become the next

Implementing AI may seem like a daunting task for small businesses, but as we've seen in these case studies, AI has the potential to drive significant improvements in customer engagement, operational efficiency, and product delivery.

The lessons learned from Ballarat Solar, Amarra, Restoke, and the Original Tamale Company prove that AI isn't just for large corporations; it can be a powerful tool for small businesses too.

Chapter 11:

The Role of Leadership in a Digital Future

Technology is only as clever as the humans guiding it.

No matter how advanced our AI tools, chatbots, or predictive dashboards get, they won't steer our business forward by themselves. A recent McKinsey study found that 70% of digital transformations fail, not because of the tech, but because people weren't on board, or the leadership fell short.[13]

Right now, we're riding a wave of rapid change. AI is rewriting the playbook on everything from customer service to supply chains. Automation is reshaping entire job roles. And market disruptions? They're popping up faster than mushrooms after rain.

Amid all this, one thing stands steady: leadership.

Tech can accelerate change, but it's leadership that gives it purpose, sets the course, and rallies people to adapt and grow. Think of it like a compass in the digital wilderness. Without strong, clear-headed leaders, even the flashiest new systems risk becoming expensive paperweights.

So as we dive deeper into this digital age, it's not just about what technology can do; it's about how we, as a leader, direct it to build a business that's agile, human, and ready for whatever comes next.

The Evolution of Leadership From Commanders to Catalysts

People don't quit companies, they quit managers who block their potential.

Not so long ago, leadership was defined by control. Picture it: strict hierarchies, corner offices, and managers who ruled with a firm hand. The boss knew best. Success was measured by how closely teams stuck to the plan, how well they executed top-down directives, and how predictably the machine ran.

In that old paradigm, employees were essentially cogs, expected to deliver on instructions, not challenge them. The culture prized loyalty, repetition, and minimising risk. Leaders focused on compliance, not creativity.

Today's digital world punishes slow movers and rewards adaptability. Customer demands change by the minute. Competitors can emerge overnight with a smarter AI tool or a more personal online experience. And new technology cycles don't wait for approval from a steering committee, they just keep coming.

That's why leadership has had to evolve, dramatically.

Old-School Leadership	Digital-Age Leadership
Top-down command & control	Empower teams to act & decide
Focus on avoiding risk	Encourage experimentation & learning
Fixed roles, rigid hierarchies	Flexible roles, flat structures
Secrecy, info on a "need-to-know"	Radical transparency & shared data
Measure inputs & hours worked	Measure outcomes & customer impact
Change only with certainty	Act decisively amid ambiguity
Reward loyalty to the status quo	Reward curiosity & challenging ideas
Leaders give answers	Leaders ask questions, remove roadblocks

From hierarchy to agility

Modern digital-age leadership flips the old pyramid on its head. Instead of rigid chains of command, today's thriving businesses operate like dynamic ecosystems:

- Teams are empowered to make decisions close to the action.
- Hierarchies are flatter, encouraging collaboration across levels.
- Feedback loops are tight and continuous, so ideas and concerns surface quickly.

In this environment, the leader's role shifts from "Commander-in-Chief" to "Chief Enabler." It's about creating the conditions; psychological safety, shared purpose, open lines of communication, where innovation can flourish and people feel energised to solve problems on their own.

Inspire and empower, don't just enforce

Instead of giving orders, today's leaders:

- Set clear, compelling visions. They paint a picture of the future that excites and aligns, giving teams a North Star to innovate towards.

- Nurture trust and ownership. They understand people thrive when they feel trusted to try, even if that means failing fast and learning.

- Foster diverse thinking. They bring together different perspectives, encourage healthy debates, and make it safe to disagree.

- Embrace transparency. In a world flooded with data and scrutiny, the best leaders share openly, about challenges, pivots, and wins.

Why this matters in the digital age

In a hyper-connected, AI-fuelled marketplace, businesses can't afford to move at the speed of managerial approval.

Decisions need to be faster. Experiments cheaper. Customer feedback looped in immediately.

And that only happens when leaders shift from controlling to catalysing. When we focus less on rigid execution and more on nurturing a culture of curiosity, courage, and continuous learning.

Because at the end of the day, no technology can compensate for a culture that's afraid to adapt.

Key Traits of Digital-Age Leaders

If technology is the rocket fuel, leaders are the navigators. And steering through the twists of a digital future calls for a different toolkit than what old-school managers carried.

Let's break down the essential traits.

Emotional Intelligence Over Ego

In times of rapid change, people don't need a hero, they need a human.

Digital transformation often brings fear: of being automated out, of learning curves, of failing publicly. Leaders who cultivate empathy and psychological safety create a climate where people feel safe to speak up, take smart risks, and admit mistakes.

What can we do as a leader?

As leaders, we can run short "pulse checks", casual chats, or 2-question surveys to see how our team's feeling. Also, share our own stumbles. A simple "I got this wrong last month. Here's what I learned" does wonders..

Vision Setting and Storytelling

Forget dry decks of quarterly targets. In a disruptive world, people rally around a compelling 'why'.

As a great digital-age leader we need to paint vivid pictures of the future, what our business will stand for, how it will delight customers, and why it matters beyond profits.

We don't just broadcast the vision; we tell stories that connect it to real people and possibilities. That way, teams can see themselves in that future.

What can we do as a leader?

At the next all-hands, tell a short story of a customer problem digital transformation will solve, then tie it to the bigger mission.

Enabling a Fail-Fast, Learn-Fast Culture

With AI, no-code tools, and ever-shifting consumer behaviours, our business must constantly experiment. That means we need a culture where small failures are celebrated as learning, not punished.

This is how we uncover what customers actually want and stay ahead of competitors.

What can we do as a leader?

We need to encourage our teams to run cheap, quick tests. Keep a visible "fail log". This is our running list of what didn't work and what was learned. It normalises experimentation.

Decisiveness in Ambiguity

The only guarantee in a digital world? Uncertainty. Customers change. Tech pivots. A competitor launches an AI feature that shifts the playing field overnight. Digital-age leaders can't afford analysis paralysis. They're comfortable making quick, data-informed calls with imperfect information, then adjusting as they learn more.

What can we do as a leader?

Use a "70% rule": If we have roughly 70% of the data or confidence, we make the call and refine on the fly.

Tech Curiosity and Lifelong Learning

No, one doesn't need to write Python scripts. But leaders who are curious about new tools and trends, who stay plugged in, make far smarter strategic bets. They also signal to their teams that learning is never optional, it's baked into the culture.

In the end, digital-age leadership is about replacing certainty with curiosity, ego with empathy, and perfection with progress. That's how we keep our business and our people, thriving.

Building Digital Trust Inside our Organisation

We can roll out the flashiest AI platform or automate half our workflows, but if our people don't trust what's happening, the whole thing will stall. Or worse, it'll backfire with silent resistance, high turnover, and a culture of whispered doubts.

Here's how modern leaders make it work.

Be transparent about digital changes, especially AI & automation

AI, bots, predictive tools are powerful, but they also trigger anxiety. Employees wonder: Will this tech replace me? Will my role even exist next year?

Leaders who hide behind buzzwords or only surface the benefits lose credibility fast. Instead, be upfront:

- Share why the team is adopting these technologies and what problems they solve for the customer and for teams.

- Explain what it means for people's roles and time. Will it free them up for more meaningful work? Will they be able to enjoy a 4-day work week, or are you just trying to do more with fewer resources? Even hard truths build more trust than sugar-coating.

- Keep the conversation going. A one-off town hall won't cut it. Make tech updates a regular drumbeat.

Involve teams in tech choices to reduce resistance

People are far more likely to back a change they helped shape. Too many digital rollouts are done to employees, not with them.

- Pilot new tools with frontline teams and gather raw feedback.
- Run "demo days" where teams can play with new tech before it's finalised.
- Use short surveys to prioritise which pain points automation should tackle first.

When people see their fingerprints on the solution, they're more invested, and the adoption hurdles drop dramatically.

Encourage cross-functional collaboration

Digital transformation rarely sits neatly in one department. AI might touch marketing, operations, and customer service, all at once. To make it work, we need to break silos and spark cross-team learning.

- Set up mixed working groups for digital initiatives, combine sales, IT, HR, even finance.
- Rotate "digital champions" across teams so they carry fresh ideas and best practices.
- Celebrate cross-department wins, like how the ops team's insight made the customer chatbot smarter.

Trust is built and earned with honest conversations, visible involvement, and shared wins. Once we do that, we will start to see the transformation roll.

How to Lead in the Digital Age

So we've seen the traits and we know the shifts. Now it's time to actually embed this into the day-to-day.

Here's a simple playbook I used to start leading in a way that made my business not just keep up with digital change, but dance with it.

Run monthly "digital debriefs"

We began by holding a casual, hour-long catch-up each month purely to explore what's happening in the business (and industry) through a digital lens.

When people know, we as leaders, expect to explore new ideas monthly, they stay switched on.

Our focus remained on three core questions:

- **What did we test lately?** Could be a new CRM feature, a social ad tweak, an AI-powered chatbot pilot.
- **What did we learn, good or bad?** No shame here. Celebrate insights, not just wins.
- **What trends are popping up in our world?** New competitor tech? Shifts in customer behaviour? Bring it in.

What can we do as a leader?

Rotate who runs it each month to spread ownership, pull in someone from another team for a fresh perspective, and keep it relaxed.

Set up cross-department innovation squads

Big, breakthrough ideas sit at the messy intersection of marketing, ops, sales, and even HR.

- So we built tiny, agile groups with people from different functions, then point them at a clear customer or workflow problem.

- **Give them a tight brief:** e.g., "How can we automate repeat customer queries by 30%?
- **Hand over a tiny budget:** enough to run quick tests or try a tool, not a giant rollout.
- **Set clear timeframes:** like four weeks, then come back and share with their learnings.

This unlocks ideas across the business, surfaces hidden rockstars, and smashes the old "that's not my department" thinking.

Build a 'fail log' to normalise learning from missteps

Want innovation to flow? Make it safe to flop.

We created a visible 'fail log', this could be a literal whiteboard in the office, a shared doc, or a dedicated chat group, where people openly list experiments that didn't work and what they learned.

- Shout them out in team meetings like we would successes.
- Praise people for taking smart risks and sharing transparently.
- Even add a cheeky "flop of the month" award to keep it playful.

When failing fast becomes ordinary, people start experimenting freely. If mistakes are hidden or punished, the smartest ideas stay trapped in someone's head.

Encourage micro-learning: 5-minute tech refreshes

Big formal courses are great, but real digital cultures grow through tiny, regular learning bites.

We found that by doing this, people stay sharp, curious, and confident tackling new tech when it's part of the everyday.

Start a weekly rhythm:
- **A 5-minute "show & tell"** where someone demos a new tool, AI feature, dashboard insight, or customer trend.
- **Rotate who does it.** It could be our junior analyst, a sales rep, or the COO.
- **Keep it totally low-stakes.**

That's how we built a business that doesn't just adapt to digital change. it thrives on it.

But let's be honest: in many ways, all of this, adapting to AI, rethinking structures, rewriting how we lead, is still about survival.

We are still trying to stay relevant in a rapidly changing world.

But what happens when we move beyond survival, toward building something that lasts, matters, and leaves a mark?

That's what's the next chapter in this book is about. But who knows, it could be the next chapter for your business, too.

Chapter 12:

From Survival to Significance – What's Next for Digital-First Businesses.

Back in 2015, digital was the lifeboat.

If you weren't online, if we didn't have some half-decent digital presence, our business was pretty much treading water, hoping not to sink while the tide of customer expectations, tech disruption, and faster competitors came crashing through.

Fast forward to 2025, and it's an entirely different ocean we're swimming in.
Being digital isn't the edge anymore, it's the starting line. It's your licence to play. The question has shifted from "How do we survive?" to "How do we shape the future we want to live in?"

Think about what we've already done across this journey:

- We've embraced AI-first thinking, letting smart systems power decisions before we even wake up.

- We've unlocked hyper-personalisation, crafting one-to-one journeys for customers who expect more than mass blasts and cookie-cutter experiences.

- We've handed the keys to innovation over to our teams, thanks to no-code and low-code tools, letting ideas turn into prototypes without waiting months for developers.

- We've built agentic systems that don't just suggest what to do, but actually do it; booking appointments, chasing leads, optimising campaigns, running your ops around the clock.

- We've embedded continuous learning into your culture so our people don't just keep up, they get ahead.

It's no small feat. We've rewired our business for the AI age. But what's all this building toward?

Is it just so we can shave another few hours off the workweek, push margins up by a point or two, or automate the next annoying admin task? Sure, those are handy. But they're not the reason we went through the slog of transformation.

Creating Enduring Value

For years, much of digital transformation was about keeping up appearances. We rushed to build fancy websites, plugged in CRMs, cranked out social content, sprinkled in a chatbot or two, and proudly ticked the digital box.

Then AI came knocking, and we thought, "Wow! This'll cut costs, automate the grunt work, maybe squeeze in a few extra bucks of margin."

All fair goals. But still, pretty tactical.

Today, tactical isn't enough. The smartest businesses have realised digital isn't just a toolkit to fix operational headaches. It's the foundation to build something bigger, something with heart, purpose and sticking power.

So what does that look like?

- It's retailers not just personalising recommendations to get another sale, but designing experiences that help people buy better, choosing local, ethical, or sustainable products.

- It's professional services firms using AI not just to optimise timesheets, but to open up more time for mentoring, creativity, and human connection.

- It's manufacturers applying predictive analytics not just to trim inventory, but to radically cut waste, carbon footprints and supply chain vulnerabilities.

In other words: shifting from "How do we extract more?" to "How do we create more value for customers, communities, and the planet?"

Because enduring value can't just be measured by quarterly earnings or another flashy campaign. It's measured by the trust we build. The problems you help solve. The legacy we leave behind.

So as we look at all these AI-first, low-code, hyper-personalised, agentic, ever-learning systems we've put in place, we need to ask ourself this:
Is my business just digital savvy, or is it significance driven?

Society, Sustainability, and the Digital-First Advantage

Being digital-first gives us a massive head start on driving positive impact.

Because unlike traditional businesses weighed down by legacy systems or slow supply chains, your digital infrastructure lets you test ideas quickly, reach customers instantly, and pivot without massive sunk costs.

Using AI & data for smarter sustainability

We've spent earlier chapters talking about AI as your new co-pilot. But there's an even bigger play: using AI and data not just to sell more, but to waste less.

Think about it:

- Predictive analytics can help keep our buildings running like clock work, when we know exactly when an HVAC might show a failure and to schedule preventive maintenance before it, minimising waste from early part replacement.

- Smart routing algorithms for dispatching technicians to job sites so as to reduce fuel consumption and carbon emissions, while also saving us money.

- Digital twins (virtual models of our buildings) let us simulate changes like IoT sensors to see the sustainability impact before you spend a cent.

Social equity & inclusion is the new digital dividend

It's easy to think of digital transformation just in terms of shiny dashboards and new revenue streams. But there's another powerful angle: access.

Digital platforms can level the playing field for groups traditionally left out.

- Think about regional Australians using online learning tailored to local industries, or small-scale farmers tapping into e-marketplaces that once would've been impossible.

- Or fintech tools helping migrants or young adults build credit histories, budget better, and avoid predatory lenders.

And when we design our systems to be inclusive from day one, ensuring our websites are accessible, our language is culturally aware, our products work on budget smartphones, we're not just ticking compliance boxes; we're unlocking whole new segments of loyal customers who are too often ignored.

The brand + customer loyalty

Customers, especially Millennials and Gen Z are actively looking for brands that stand for something more. They'll pay more, stay longer, and recommend us widely if they believe we're genuinely out to make a difference.

Sharing our impact stories, through social content, dashboards on our website, even cheeky packaging copy, gives people reasons to feel proud buying from you. The same goes for our team: people want to work for companies doing meaningful things, not just chasing the next quarterly target.

Slowly, but surely, our sustainability initiatives, coupled with our digital-first mindset, begin to add up towards better loyalty, better talent, and better margins.

Weaving Tech with Trust as we Scale

As we get further in our digital transformation journey with AI models running predictions, personalised campaigns firing automatically, and low-code platforms letting our team whip up new tools in days, there remains one hard truth: none of it matters if customers, employees, or partners don't trust what we're doing.

Scaling up without trust is like building a high-rise on sand. Eventually, cracks show. Data leaks, biased algorithms, or dodgy privacy practices can do more than hurt our reputation; they can wipe out years of hard-won loyalty overnight.

Building ethics into our scaling blueprint

Responsible growth means asking the harder questions upfront.

- Are our AI models transparent and explainable? If a customer asks why they were declined for an offer, or shown a particular product, can we give them a clear, fair answer?

- Is our personalisation respectful, or a bit creepy? Hyper-targeted ads are clever until they cross a line that makes people feel surveilled rather than served.

- How secure is our customer data? From sign-ups to transactions to post-sale service, privacy needs to be built in, not bolted on.

- Are we thinking inclusively? That means not just accessibility, but also ensuring our algorithms aren't reinforcing biases that sideline certain groups.

When we embed these checks into our scaling plan, it stops being just about risk avoidance. it becomes a real point of differentiation. People buy from, work for, and champion businesses they trust.

Keeping our people & partners aligned

Trust also starts at home. Our team needs to understand our ethics as deeply as our tech stack. That means regular training on data privacy, AI ethics, and inclusive design, not as dry compliance sessions, but as core to who we are.

Same goes for partners. If we're outsourcing development or data processing, do those vendors live up to your standards? Because at the end of the day, our customers see them as an extension of us.

Society, Sustainability, and the Digital-First Advantage

Let's face it, the digital world can get a bit obsessed with the next big thing. One day it's AI chat, next it's virtual reality showrooms, then it's NFTs, and on it goes. But chasing trends for the sake of it is like redecorating the house every month while ignoring the dodgy foundations. It might look fresh, but it doesn't last.

The businesses that stand out are the ones that innovate with a clear eye on legacy. They pick tools and projects that align with who they are, what they value, and what they want to be remembered for.

This is where you need to align tech with purpose:

It's time to ask ourselves:

- Does this new tool or product line actually serve our mission?
- Will it matter to our customers and to us in five or ten years?
- Is it making lives easier, healthier, more sustainable, or more connected in ways that align with your brand?

That doesn't mean we stop experimenting.

Being digitally mature means we can test new ideas quickly and cheaply. It means we can be playful. We just filter our experiments through the question: "Will this build towards the kind of legacy we want?"

Not every pilot will turn into a core offering, and that's fine. But over time, we'll have a portfolio of innovations that all stack up towards something more meaningful than just quarterly gains.

Shaping a Culture of Significance

In the previous chapter we discussed how digital transformation often starts at the top, it needs leadership vision, budget, and willingness to take risks. But building a business that moves from mere survival to long-term significance is something our entire team has to live and breathe.

From continuous learning to meaningful growth

Earlier in this book, we explored how fostering continuous learning is essential to keep pace with change. But this next evolution is about learning with purpose.

It's not just upskilling so people can wrangle the latest tool or platform. It's about helping them see how their daily work ladders up to bigger goals, whether that's cutting waste, empowering communities, or shaping a more inclusive marketplace.

Imagine the power of a team where:

- Developers aren't just coding features, they're building platforms that improve lives.

- Marketing team isn't just running campaigns; they're sharing stories of how our solutions solve real-world problems.

- Customer support isn't just closing tickets, they're champions of trust and transparency.

Bringing our people into the "why"

So how do we actually create this culture of significance?

Start by making it a two-way conversation. It's not enough to stick our purpose on a wall and hope people buy in. Bring our teams together and ask:

- "What are we proud of in the work we do?"

- "Where do you see us making the biggest difference?"

- "What impact would we love to say we had in 10 years' time?"

We might be surprised by the ideas that bubble up, or by how much more our people care about these bigger goals than quarterly KPIs.

Leading by living it

Of course, none of this sticks if leadership isn't modelling it daily.

Our managers and execs need to make decisions that show legacy matters more than just quick wins. They need to praise teams for work that advances your mission, not just work that closes another deal.

It's about being the kind of organisation where someone can say:

"I chose to work here because I wanted to help build something meaningful. And every day, I feel like we're actually doing that."

A culture that's driven by significance becomes its own competitive advantage. It fuels innovation, it attracts brilliant people who care about more than a paycheck, and it keeps customers coming back not just for your products, but because of what you stand for.

So take the time to nurture it.

Let's embed it in how we hire, how we recognise success, how we set goals, and where we invest. Because in the end, building a culture of significance is all about building a business that truly lasts.

Chapter 13:

Real Insights from the AI Frontier

If there is one thing the 2025 Global CIO & CISO Summit in Colombo, Sri Lanka made clear, it's that AI is no longer just a supporting tool but a defining force in business transformation.

Surrounded by some of the brightest AI leaders, innovators, and disrupters, I witnessed firsthand how bold ideas are rapidly moving from concept to reality. The summit didn't just validate my ideas on digital transformation; it propelled them further, opening my eyes to the extraordinary potential of startups that are crafting the future right now.

During the summit, I had the privilege of connecting with some of these pioneering startup founders who came from Canada, India, Sri Lanka, Switzerland, the UK, and the USA. Our conversations were rich, candid, and forward-looking. What struck me most was their willingness to share not just their innovations, but also the values and principles guiding their work.

These exchanges inspired me to capture their insights in this chapter, so SMEs everywhere can learn directly from the people building the AI future.

Because one thing is for sure. AI is no longer a distant concept reserved for Silicon Valley giants. Across the globe, ambitious startups are reimagining how small and medium-sized enterprises (SMEs) can work smarter, grow faster, and serve customers better.

This chapter will help us see not just what is coming, but how to prepare for it, right from founders who are living at the edge of innovation, testing bold ideas, solving real-world problems, and shaping what the AI-powered SME of tomorrow will look like.

Startups in the Spotlight

As we look ahead, these innovative startups are leading the charge in AI for SMEs. Each of them is reshaping industries and proving that AI can be a powerful ally in creating smarter, more efficient businesses.

Care41

Care41 is an AI-powered senior care platform that combines AI and human oversight for proactive, personalised care. It enables real-time collaboration between caregivers, doctors, and families. Care41 uses AI to scale caregiving while maintaining the human touch.

FirstHive

FirstHive is an Intelligent Customer Data Platform powered by agentic AI. Their Eddie platform doesn't just analyse, it autonomously runs campaigns and personalises customer journeys, all with a privacy-first, GDPR-compliant design.

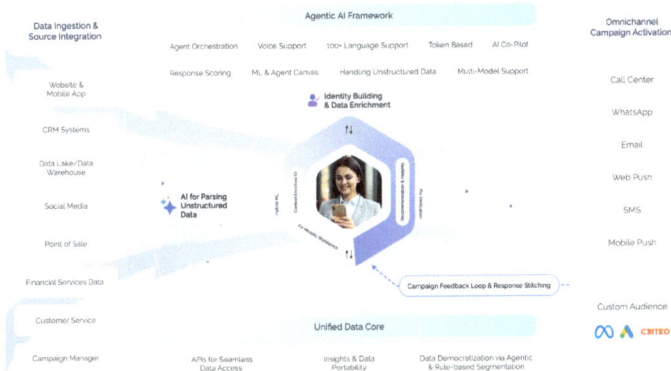

Hivel

PR Alpha by Sean is **750+ LoC** and unreviewed for 8 days. Break this PR into smaller parts and **assign** them to Reviewers Penelope and Spencer for a quick review.

Hivel is an AI-first startup that enhances engineering workflows with an intelligence layer for real-time action and risk identification. Their solutions help SMEs accelerate development and boost efficiency. Hivel envisions AI as a trusted teammate, not just a tool.

TechCrafter

TechCrafter provides AI-powered solutions to SMEs in MedTech, Mobility, and Manufacturing, focusing on democratising AI for smaller businesses. Their tools streamline operations and improve productivity. TechCrafter helps SMEs compete globally through AI innovation.

Thunai

Thunai AI offers agentic AI middleware that unifies fragmented systems into a cohesive, intelligent whole. With agents that automate workflows and resolve over 60% of Tier 1 support tickets, Thunai helps SMEs scale fast without losing the human touch.

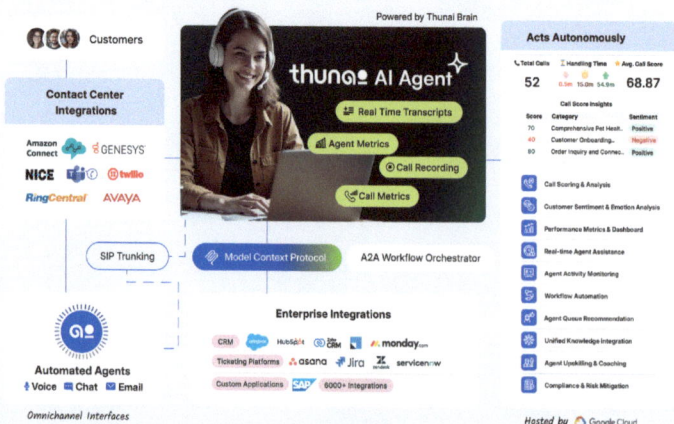

Trupeer AI

Trupeer AI is building a "second brain" for organisations, turning raw information into accessible, shareable knowledge. From videos to searchable knowledge bases, Trupeer helps SMEs stay sharp, organised, and always-on.

Joboro AI

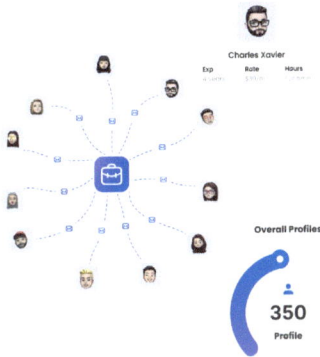

Joboro AI is reimagining recruitment. From AI-powered CV analysis to voice/video candidate screening, Joboro helps businesses hire smarter, faster, and fairer, reducing bias while keeping human judgment at the centre.

Note: While Joboro AI was not part of the 2025 Global CIO & CISO Summit in Colombo, their insights and innovations have been included for their valuable contribution to SME-focused AI solutions.

The Future Trends SMEs Can't Ignore

The pace of AI innovation can feel dizzying, but for SMEs it represents one of the greatest opportunities in decades. What once seemed futuristic is now practical, affordable, and within reach.

The startup founders I spoke with shared not just predictions, but actionable trends that are already reshaping how small businesses work, sell, and serve customers. Their perspectives reveal where the market is heading and how SMEs can ride this wave instead of being swept aside.

Democratisation of AI Levels the Playing Field

Care41 views the democratisation of AI as one of the most powerful trends for small and medium-sized businesses (SMEs). Traditionally, AI was seen as a luxury only accessible to large corporations with the resources to invest in complex models, infrastructure, and R&D.

For instance, an SME in healthcare, like Care41, could use AI tools to offer personalized care recommendations for elderly people, help doctors provide timely insights, and track health data effectively. These capabilities were once reserved for hospitals with huge budgets and technical expertise.

As a result, AI becomes a competitive advantage, not just for the big players but for anyone willing to adopt and leverage it wisely.

AI-powered Process Automation

TechCrafter highlights that AI-powered process automation is one of the strongest trends SMEs should adopt. From back-office tasks like invoice processing, compliance, and HR to shop-floor scheduling and logistics, AI-driven bots and digital twins will help SMEs reduce waste and boost efficiency.

AI is already saving small logistics companies up to 20% on fuel costs with route optimisation, while MedTech SMEs are using AI-assisted radiology to analyse X-rays faster and more reliably. By embracing these automation trends, SMEs can reduce overheads, increase productivity, and scale faster than before.

From Automation to Autonomy

FirstHive believes the next era of AI will be defined by agentic systems, AI agents that not only predict behaviour but also act on it. Their Eddie platform demonstrates how autonomous marketing agents can independently design campaigns, generate dynamic content, and manage customer journeys.

This shift from automation to autonomy represents a seismic leap: instead of humans pushing buttons, AI will proactively optimise outcomes, freeing SMEs to focus on higher-order strategy. Think of it as moving from having an assistant to having an entire marketing department that never sleeps.

AI Agents as the New Workforce

"SMEs should embrace AI not as software but as teammates", the founder of Joboro AI says.

By handling CV screening, audio/video interviews, and candidate scoring, AI takes on the heavy lifting of recruitment while HR teams focus on building authentic connections with candidates.

Of course, this mindset, seeing AI as part of the team, extends beyond hiring.

For SMEs, this means deploying AI "workforces" that resolve customer queries, schedule appointments, qualify leads, handle transactions, and automate routine operations 24/7 without needing large teams.

The SMEs that succeed will be those who treat AI as a trusted colleague, not just a cost-saving tool.

Personalisation as Self-Expression

Trupeer AI believes the future lies in turning users into marketers of themselves. "It is not about who made the best software - it's about who makes the user look the best," reflects Trupeer's founder.

AI should empower customers to express who they are, whether through personalised product recommendations, email marketing, financial advice, or adaptive interfaces.

With generative tools, small teams can compete with enterprise-level creative output, producing high-quality, customised content at speed and scale.

Multimodal AI at Scale

Thunai believes multimodal AI will change the game for SMEs drowning in scattered knowledge.

By processing diverse inputs like documents, audio, video, chat logs, AI can unify fragmented data into actionable insights.

For example, imagine a service business where AI automatically summarises a client meeting, generates follow-up emails, and updates the CRM, all within minutes. This ability to centralise and operationalise knowledge turns SMEs into lean, insight-driven organisations that compete effectively with much larger players.

Shift From Dashboards to Intelligence Layers

Businesses are moving beyond traditional dashboards that simply display data and metrics. Instead, AI will evolve into an intelligent layer that not only tracks data but actively interprets it, making it actionable in real-time.

Hivel envisions this as a next-level shift where AI doesn't just report the numbers or trends but also suggests actions, highlights potential risks, and offers insights into how to improve processes.

This shift from just tracking to proactively collaborating is especially for teams working in dynamic environments. Instead of spending time deciphering metrics, teams will be able to focus on creative solutions and innovation, with AI providing the groundwork for faster, smarter forecasting, personalisation, and decision-making. In essence, AI becomes a co-worker that enhances human capabilities, accelerating the pace and accuracy of work.

Key Takeaway: The future belongs to SMEs who treat AI as an extension of their team; always-on, multi-skilled, and ready to learn. Autonomous systems, multimodal intelligence, and hyper-personalisation will redefine competitiveness.

The Ethical Guardrails for AI Adoption

With great power comes great responsibility. Today's tech leaders stress that ethics must guide adoption, not as a box-ticking exercise, but as the bedrock of sustainable growth.

For SMEs, ethics in AI isn't just about staying out of trouble with regulators. It's about building the kind of trust that keeps customers loyal, investors confident, and employees motivated. Without this foundation, even the smartest AI solutions risk crumbling under the weight of mistrust or misuse.

Privacy First

FirstHive believes "customer trust begins with data privacy." Their platform is designed with a GDPR-compliant, privacy-first architecture.

For SMEs, this means never treating customer data as a disposable asset; it's a sacred trust.

Privacy must extend beyond policies into daily practices: securing consent before collecting information, storing it responsibly, and giving customers control over how their data is used.

TechCrafter and others agree: "Data is the lifeblood of AI, but using it without consent or mishandling it can erode trust."

Beyond compliance, privacy-first AI builds loyalty, reduces regulatory risk, and positions your brand as responsible and future-ready.

Bias Prevention

Thunai AI stresses that "AI must be actively monitored for bias and fairness." Left unchecked, algorithms can perpetuate systemic inequalities and damage brand credibility.

Thunai combats this by tailoring models to high-quality, domain-specific knowledge rather than generic datasets.

TechCrafter also highly seconds this critical ethical pillar. "AI systems are only as good as the data that feeds them. If training data carries historical or social bias, AI will replicate and even amplify these biases."

For SMEs, this lesson is clear: train AI on data that reflects your real customers, not the noisy, biased internet at large. This approach ensures fairer outcomes in recruitment, marketing, and service delivery, while protecting businesses from reputational and even legal risks.

Transparency and Explainability

A common theme that echoed across all founder responses was the "Why" behind AI responses.

According to Joboro AI, "explainable AI is essential to accountability." Hiven calls it "Transparency over black boxes".

Customers deserve to know why a product recommendation was made, why their loan was denied, or why they were shortlisted for a job.

Without transparency, trust quickly erodes. SMEs should adopt tools that log AI decisions, provide clear reasoning, and allow humans to review and refine them. By doing so, businesses not only reassure customers but also empower teams to learn from the system's logic and continuously improve outcomes.

Human Oversight

Despite what AI has to offer, it's the people who must remain accountable. Trupeer, Joboro, FirstHive, and Thunai each emphasised the value of human-in-the-loop systems.

"AI should be a part of the process, not the final call taker," says Hivel.

AI may execute, but people must oversee. For SMEs, this means defining clear lines of responsibility: who steps in when AI falters, and how they intervene? Establishing protocols for handovers ensures that machines don't make unchecked decisions in moments that require human empathy, judgment, or nuance.

Redefining Roles

While AI automation can streamline operations, it also carries the risk of displacing roles, particularly in customer-facing functions. This is a pressing concern for SMEs whose staff often wear multiple hats and may feel vulnerable to automation.

Thuanai AI believes the solution to "preserving jobs is to redefine roles around it. By focusing on upskilling employees, SMEs can turn AI into a tool for augmentation rather than replacement."

Agentic AI, for example, can handle routine queries or repetitive workflows, freeing teams to focus on strategic tasks such as building customer relationships or designing new offerings. This approach enhances human productivity, helping SMEs grow without large-scale layoffs.

Sustainability

Thunai AI, reminds us that "the energy footprint of AI is an often-ignored ethical issue. Lightweight, efficient models not only cut costs but also reduce environmental impact."

As SMEs adopt AI, sustainability should sit alongside performance in the decision-making process. Cloud providers with green credentials, efficient model architectures, and optimised infrastructure aren't just eco-friendly—they're cost-effective too. SMEs that align with green practices can future-proof their operations and build goodwill with increasingly eco-conscious customers.

Key Takeaway: Ethical AI isn't just about compliance; it's about building trust. SMEs that prioritise privacy, fairness, transparency, oversight, and sustainability will gain long-term loyalty.

Keeping the Human Touch Alive

The consistent message from these founders is clear: AI should enable empathy, not erase it.

TechCrafter puts it beautifully: "One of the paradoxes of the digital age is that the more technology pervades our lives, the more people long for authentic human connections. SMEs often thrive on personal trust, community reputation, and close customer relationships; so must balance this carefully. Adopting AI does not mean sacrificing the human touch, in fact, when applied thoughtfully, AI can free up human capacity to deepen empathy, personalisation and trust."

While technology can deliver scale, efficiency, and insights at levels humans can't match, it is still people who bring warmth and understanding to every interaction. For SMEs, the challenge is not whether to adopt AI, but how to do so in a way that strengthens human connection rather than diluting it.

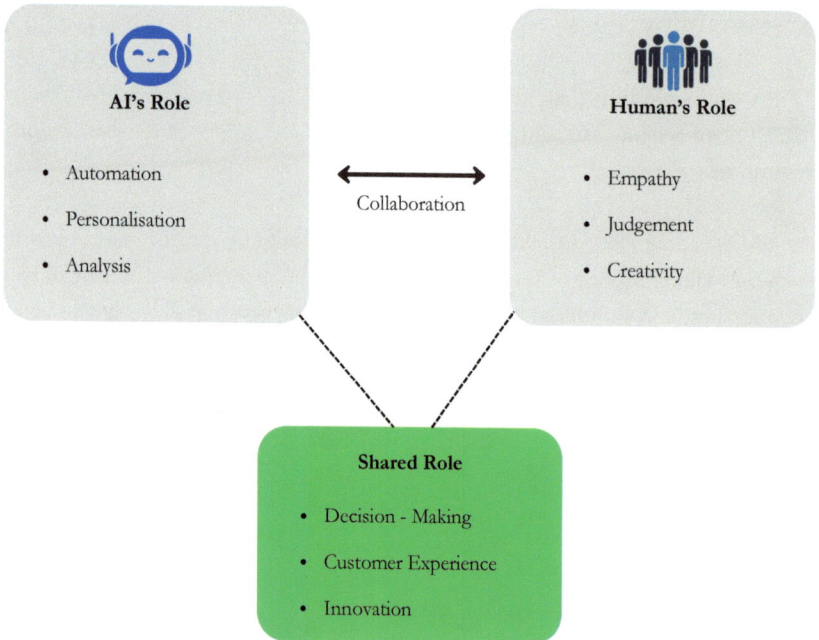

AI's Role

- Automation
- Personalisation
- Analysis

Collaboration

Human's Role

- Empathy
- Judgement
- Creativity

Shared Role

- Decision - Making
- Customer Experience
- Innovation

Hybrid Systems

Thunai AI believes SMEs should implement hybrid AI-human models. In this approach, AI handles FAQs or Tier 1 support, such as password resets, order tracking, or routine troubleshooting, while humans step in for complex or emotionally sensitive issues.

Thunai's own platform demonstrates this balance, with agents autonomously resolving 61% of Tier 1 tickets and seamlessly escalating the rest to human staff. This model ensures speed and availability without losing humanity.

For SMEs, it means customers get instant support when they need it most, but still receive empathetic, human care in moments of frustration or nuance. It's not just about efficiency; it's about ensuring that technology never becomes a cold barrier between business and customer.

AI-Enabled Empathy

FirstHive enhances empathy by delivering 1:1 personalisation at scale.

Their platform analyses customer touchpoints in real time, enabling businesses to anticipate needs and craft responses that feel individually tailored. Imagine an SME retailer knowing, in the moment, that a loyal customer is at risk of churn and offering a personalised discount or heartfelt message that rekindles trust.

The power here is not in replacing human warmth, but in giving teams the intelligence to act with greater empathy.

When customers feel understood, they are not just satisfied; they feel valued. This emotional connection is what builds loyalty that lasts beyond a single transaction. Hivel seconds this: "The real opportunity is to treat AI as the backstage crew, efficient, invisible, and powerful, while humans remain center stage, delivering the authenticity customers will always value."

Human-in-the-Loop for High-Impact Decisions

Joboro AI says that while AI can shortlist candidates or draft responses, final judgment must remain human.

In recruitment, for example, AI can narrow down hundreds of applications, but it cannot fully grasp cultural fit, subtle cues, or potential. Similarly, in customer-facing contexts, AI might draft responses or flag insights, but humans bring the nuance needed to handle delicate situations.

This hybrid approach ensures fairness while leveraging AI for speed and efficiency. SMEs can save countless hours while still safeguarding against the risks of leaving high-stakes decisions entirely to machines.

Design Human-Centric Experiences

The adoption of AI should be guided by design thinking. "Start with the customer's emotional journey, then imbibe AI," says TechCrafter.

In healthcare, patients want reassurance and empathy. AI can accelerate diagnosis, but the "last mile" delivery must be human-to-human. In logistics, clients want timely updates. AI can automate shipment tracking, but delivery staff can build goodwill through courteous, personalised service.

Technology should be invisible; the experience should feel human.

AI to Solve, Not Delegate

Care41 believes that AI should be seen as a problem-solving partner, assisting humans in making better decisions rather than just executing instructions.

For instance, AI can analyse patient data to identify early warning signs in healthcare, suggest personalised care plans, or flag critical incidents. Humans then interpret, validate, and act on these insights.

This approach ensures that AI supports human judgment rather than displacing it, making decisions more informed, timely, and context-aware.

Empowering Users

Trupeer AI sees AI's potential in making customers feel like the heroes of their own story.

Trupeer transforms raw information into shareable, personalised formats that amplify how users see themselves. From getting their problems solved to standing out in what they do; that's the journey customers want to take.

This philosophy shifts the focus from business-driven outcomes to customer-driven experiences. When AI empowers customers to express themselves, achieve more, or feel smarter, it deepens emotional engagement.

For SMEs, this can be the difference between a one-off buyer and a lifelong advocate.

Key Takeaway
The businesses that thrive will be those that let AI amplify empathy. Scale and efficiency are vital, but warmth and authenticity remain irreplaceable.

Human-Centred, AI-Powered

When I first stepped into the 2025 Global CIO & CISO Summit in Colombo, I expected lots of talk about algorithms, platforms, and new tools. And yes, there was plenty of that. But what struck me most wasn't the tech; it was the people behind it.

These startup founders weren't just coding products; they were shaping philosophies about trust, empathy, and how businesses can thrive without losing their human touch.

That's the real story here.

The future isn't about AI taking over and pushing people aside. It's about AI giving us the space and the tools to do what we do best: connect with each other, think creatively, and build meaningful relationships.

AI can crunch numbers faster than any of us, work through the night without complaint, and handle the routine stuff that bogs teams down. But it can't laugh with our customers, feel their frustrations, or share in their wins. That part? That will always belong to humans.

For SMEs, that's great news. It means we don't need to compete with machines; we get to collaborate with them. By weaving ethics and empathy into how we adopt the emerging AI trends, we can grow smarter and kinder.

By helping our teams work alongside AI, we can boost productivity without losing jobs or trust. And by using AI to really understand our customers, we can serve them in ways that feel genuine and personal.

Chapter 14:

Building a Business That Adapts, Learns, and Leads

Let's take a moment to breathe this in: our business is not the same as it was a decade ago.

More importantly, we're not the same.

Back in 2015, most businesses approached digital like an insurance policy. Get online so we wouldn't be left behind. Try some social media posts. Maybe test a bit of e-commerce or automation. It was about survival; keeping pace with shifting customer expectations and avoiding the slow fade into irrelevance. But now look at what we're building.

Across this book, we haven't just ticked off a list of new tools. We've been rewiring how we see business itself.

- We've stopped viewing AI as some shiny toy, and instead put it at the centre of our decisions, anticipating customer needs, guiding operations, and unlocking opportunities our competitors can't even see.

- We've shifted from one-size-fits-all to hyper-personalisation, treating each customer as a story, not just a statistic.

- We've broken through old bottlenecks, empowering our people to create solutions on their own through no-code and low-code platforms, building a culture where innovation isn't someone else's job.

- We've welcomed agentic systems, letting AI act on our behalf, so our business can run 24/7, without burning out our teams.

- We've moved beyond static playbooks to embrace continuous learning, turning our whole organisation into a living system that grows smarter every day.

- And we've discovered that true leadership in this new world isn't about having all the answers. It's about asking better questions, setting clear ethical lines, and inspiring people to rally around a purpose bigger than quarterly gains.

Business transformation strategies

Shift from one-size-fits-all to hyper-personalisation, valuing customer stories
Hyper-personal customer approach

Welcome agentic systems for 24/7 business operation, preventing team burnout
Adopt agentic AI systems

True leadership involves better questions, ethics, and inspiring purpose over gains
Redefine leadership purpose

AI central decision-making

AI is central to decisions, anticipating needs and unlocking unique opportunities

Empower innovation via no-code

Empower teams through no-code/low-code platforms to foster innovation culture

Embrace continuous learning

Move beyond static playbooks to continuous learning, evolving the organisation daily

Most powerfully, we've begun to pivot from simply surviving disruption to driving significance, shaping a business that doesn't just make money, but makes a difference. One that our customers trust, our employees feel proud of, and our community sees as a genuine force for good.

Because here's the deeper truth: this journey isn't just about upgrading our systems. It's about upgrading our ambition.

It's about deciding that our business will be one of those rare stories people tell in ten, twenty, fifty years, because we used tech to build something that mattered. And that's why this isn't the end of our transformation.

It's just the start of a much bigger chapter, one where we keep learning, keep adapting, and keep leading boldly into whatever comes next.

The new rules of the game

Here's what's crystal clear after this journey: digital is no longer something we "do on the side." It's not a department, a line item, or a temporary campaign.

It's the very operating system of our business.

Everything, from how we find customers to how we keep them, how we hire and grow our people, how we spot threats and seize opportunities, is now built on a digital backbone.

But here's the catch: the rules have changed.

It's no longer enough to just be tech-savvy. Or to automate for efficiency. Or to chase the next platform trend hoping it gives you a quick lift.

Today's winners, and tomorrow's legends understand that digital isn't just a set of tools. It's a philosophy. A mindset. It's how we approach every challenge, every growth plan, every customer promise.

It means:

- Designing systems that learn and evolve, not just execute static processes.

- Personalising experiences so deeply they feel tailor-made for every individual who interacts with our brand.

- Using AI and automation to free up human creativity, not replace it.

- Building agile teams that see change not as a disruption to endure, but as fuel for new ideas.

- And weaving trust, ethics, and purpose into every digital decision, so we're moving right.

Because in this new game, speed and scale are only half the story. It's the ability to learn faster than the world changes that separates the good from the truly great.

So as we close out this book, hold on to this: our biggest competitive edge isn't any single tool or framework we've covered. It's your capacity to keep learning, adapting, and reinventing, again and again.

That's the heart of this next era. And it's ours for the taking.

Why learning faster than change is our ultimate advantage

If there's one truth that's become impossible to ignore, it's this: Change isn't slowing down.

New technologies, market disruptions, shifting customer expectations, global shocks, they don't arrive on a neat schedule. They pile up, collide, and spark entirely new realities. What felt cutting-edge last year might be table stakes today, or even obsolete tomorrow.

So what separates businesses that thrive from those that fade?

It's not who has the biggest budget or the most patents. It's not who jumped on the latest shiny tech first.

It's who learns faster. Who adapts faster. Who can spot signals in the noise and pivot while others are still debating the slide deck.

We've already seen this playing out in industries all around you:

- Retailers who treated online as an afterthought were crushed by those who built seamless hybrid experiences.

- Health providers who scrambled to bolt on telehealth are now chasing patient loyalty from nimble startups that made remote care effortless from day one.

- Local trades like plumbers, sparkies, landscaping crews are now running smarter than ever, using AI-powered job management software that handles booking, messaging, and scheduling automatically, while traditional operators wrestle paper diaries and endless phone tags.

- Property managers are streamlining entire portfolios with automated work order systems, AI-driven supplier selection, and predictive maintenance, keeping tenants happier, cutting downtime, and protecting asset value, all while their old-school rivals drown in spreadsheets and reactive repairs.

The point isn't to fear this. It's to get excited. Because as a digital-first business, we already have the muscles for this kind of rapid learning. We've implemented AI, empowered our people with low-code, woven continuous upskilling into our culture. We're not starting from zero. We're already running.

Now it's about doubling down. Making sure our systems are designed to learn. That our teams see change as an opportunity to test, explore, and grow. That we celebrate smart failures as much as big wins, because each one teaches us how to be better.

Because here's the ultimate play: in a world where change never stops, being a business that learns faster than change itself isn't just an advantage, it's survival. And more than that, it's our pathway to lasting significance.

Building a Business That Adapts, Learns, and Leads

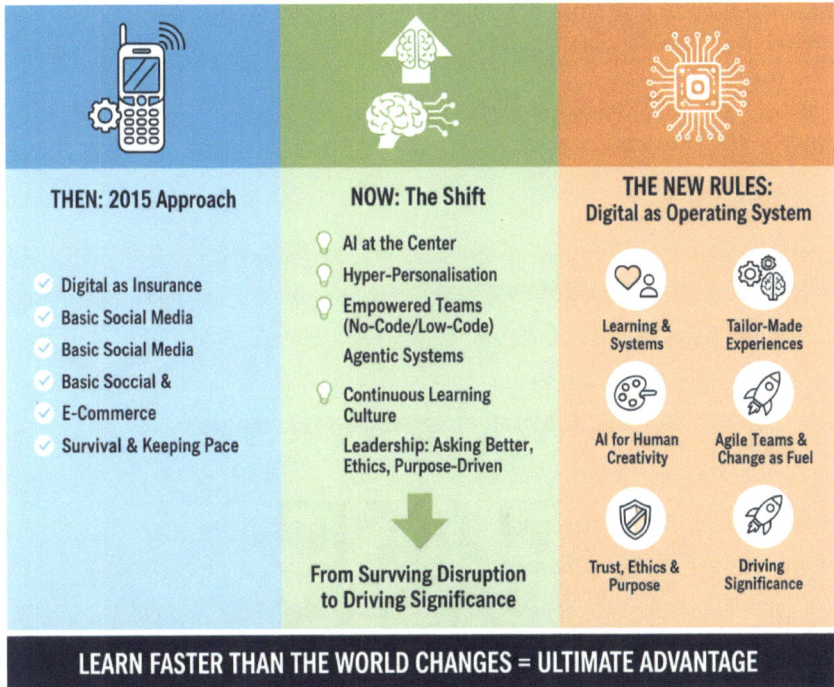

THEN: 2015 Approach

- Digital as Insurance
- Basic Social Media
- Basic Social Media
- Basic Soccial &
- E-Commerce
- Survival & Keeping Pace

NOW: The Shift

- AI at the Center
- Hyper-Personalisation
- Empowered Teams (No-Code/Low-Code)
- Agentic Systems
- Continuous Learning Culture
- Leadership: Asking Better, Ethics, Purpose-Driven

From Survving Disruption to Driving Significance

THE NEW RULES: Digital as Operating System

Learning & Systems

Tailor-Made Experiences

AI for Human Creativity

Agile Teams & Change as Fuel

Trust, Ethics & Purpose

Driving Significance

LEARN FASTER THAN THE WORLD CHANGES = ULTIMATE ADVANTAGE

Retail: Seamless Hybrid   Healthcars: AI Job Management   Local Trades: Management: Predictive Maintenance

Let's build our future

So here we are, at the end of this book, but really, standing right at the starting line of our next chapter.

The truth is, the future doesn't belong to those who stand still and wait to see what happens.

It belongs to those who roll up their sleeves, get curious, keep experimenting, keep evolving, faster than change itself.

Those who lead not with fear, but with boldness, ethics, and heart.

So take everything we've explored here and put it into practice. Run pilots, test wild ideas, build trust, nurture people, tell impact stories, keep refining the "why."

Stay restless, stay humble, stay hungry to learn.

Because the biggest opportunities are still ahead.

So go on.
Go build your future.

Not just a business that thrives today, but one that's ready to keep learning, adapting, and leading for whatever tomorrow brings.

i4T Global's journey as it unfolds

References

[1] Nathan, L. (2015). Think Digital – The Ultimate Digital Transformation Guide for SMEs. Retrieved from: https://www.amazon.com/Ultimate-Digital-Transformation-Guide/dp/1514770660

[2] Canva. (2024). AI Assistant. Retrieved from: https://www.canva.com/ai-assistant/?

[3] Enreap. (2024). Atlassian Rovo: AI-driven insights for high-performing teams. Retrieved from: https://enreap.com/atlassian-rovo-ai-driven-insights-for-high-performing-teams/#:~:text=Atlassian%20Rovo%20is%20an%20intelligent,spent%20searching%20for%20critical%20data

[4] Think with Google. (n.d.). Micro-Moments: Understanding new consumer behaviour. Retrieved from: https://www.thinkwithgoogle.com/consumer-insights/consumer-journey/micro-moments-understand-new-consumer-behavior/

[5] Mayple. (n.d.). Koala case study. Retrieved from: https://www.mayple.com/resources/email-marketing/koala-case-study

[6] Holini. (n.d.). HealthMatch case study. Retrieved from: https://holini.com/case-studies/healthmatch/

[7] Yotpo. (n.d.). Frank Body case study. Retrieved from: https://www.yotpo.com/case-studies/lucent-globe-case-study/

[8] Marr, B. (2024, November 22). The AI-powered citizen revolution: How every employee is becoming a technology creator. Forbes. Retrieved from: https://www.forbes.com/sites/bernardmarr/2024/11/22/the-ai-powered-citizen-revolution-how-every-employee-is-becoming-a-technology-creator/

[9] Business Insider. (2024). Wholesale formal gown distributor using AI for e-commerce operations. Retrieved from: https://www.businessinsider.com/wholesale-formal-gown-distributor-using-ai-for-ecommerce-operations

[10] The Australian. (2024). Melbourne startup Restoke AI says it's saving restaurants $8,000 a week, sparking a global revolution. Retrieved from: https://www.theaustralian.com.au/business/technology/melbourne-startup-restoke-ai-says-its-saving-restaurants-8000-a-week-sparking-a-global-revolution/news-story/49fa80c151014a4f5e6dfddd2987ee0f

[11] The Business Insider. (2025). The Original Tamale Company's viral AI video shows small businesses can leverage artificial intelligence to go big online. Retrieved from https://www.businessinsider.com/the-original-tamale-company-los-angeles-viral-ai-video-2025-8

[12] McKinsey & Company. (2023). Unlocking success in digital transformations. Retrieved from: https://www.mckinsey.com/capabilities/people-and-organizational-performance/our-insights/unlocking-success-in-digital-transformations

Appendices

This page expands on the ideas in the book with fresh
AI resources, examples, and discussions.

Scan. Explore. Evolve.

Think Digital
Rewired for the AI Age

APPENDICES

Chapter 02	**AI Toolkit** Practical tools to begin embedding intelligence into your business.	>
Chapter 03	**Prompts Cheatsheet** Learn to ask better questions for hyper-personalisation.	>
Chapter 04	Low-Code Tools Guide	

www.ingramcontent.com/pod-product-compliance
Lightning Source LLC
Chambersburg PA
CBHW041006210326

41597CB00006B/148